Graziella Roccella

GIO PONTI

1891–1979

Master of Lightness

TASCHEN

HONG KONG KÖLN LONDON LOS ANGELES MADRID PARIS TOKYO

Illustration page 2 ▶ Gio Ponti in Caracas,
Venezuela, 1953
Illustration page 4 ▶ The architect, drawing
commissioned by the Richard-Ginori Company

©2009 TASCHEN GmbH
Hohenzollernring 53, D-50672 Köln
www.taschen.com

Editor ▶ Peter Gössel, Bremen
Project management ▶ Katrin Schumann,
Eva Rietschel, Bremen
Design and layout ▶ Gössel und Partner, Bremen
Text edited by ▶ Johannes Althoff, Berlin
Translation ▶ Wolfgang Mann, Sydney, and
William Hatherell, Brisbane
Editorial coordination ▶ Johannes Althoff, Berlin

Printed in Germany
ISBN 978-3-8365-0038-8

Contents

Introduction

Ceramic designs by Ponti

Opposite Page:
Fresco in the stairwell of the Palazzo Bo, University of Padua, 1940
These frescos provided an opportunity for Ponti to express himself as a painter. The curved surface shows different figures symbolising the faculties of a university.

Gio Ponti was the epitome of Homo Ludens (man the player). He drew and designed tirelessly, deep into the night, in trains, aeroplanes, and even in the car. He was rarely seen without paper and pencil. He devoted himself to architecture and painting, as well as to design and interior decoration. In all these fields he achieved an authentic voice: whatever he touched turned into genuine Ponti.

If he had been asked what was for him the perfect shape, Ponti would have referred to the obelisk, which he once characterised as "the true and pure symbol of architectural expression". For Ponti the obelisk was "an enigma": "The obelisk, sibylline and metaphysical ... represents an arcane, non-functional ... architecture; the pure, the only plastic act, the accent." The obelisk can be seen as the symbol for Ponti's artistic striving for the utmost clarity of shape, to ensure balance through harmony and beauty: "The obelisk stands in a dangerous equilibrium, at the brink of balance. We fear that it may fall and consider it a miracle that it stands. Its base must be as small as possible; its height, as great as possible." Such an emphasis on balance shows the degree to which Ponti was indebted to the classical canon.

Ponti had a strong affinity with the obelisk. He used it, for example, to decorate his very first building at Via Randaccio in Milan. His dealings with the obelisk also reveal the changing relation of Ponti's architecture to the Modern. One could say that he transformed the obelisk. Such a transformation found its fullest expression in what is probably Ponti's most famous building, the Pirelli Tower in Milan. Here he and his friend, engineer Pier Luigi Nervi, spent many hours of painstaking detailed work to liberate the building from any superfluous weight so that it fulfilled the condition of equilibrium.

Ponti viewed his position as an artist in the sense of the idealised image of an artist of the 19th century, as a mediator between the spheres of ideas and reality. He followed his genius and was an initiator of excellence. This stance also dominates his working method in a narrower sense: he always had collaborators executing his ideas. The motive of the angel that Ponti often used can be read as symbolic of his own conception of himself as a mediator: he not only gave its name to one of his first houses *L'Ange Volant* (The Flying Angel), but also fitted the windows of his last apartment at Via Dezza with angel figures.

Ponti also played a role in mediating between different times, between tradition and the Modern. Equipped with a tremendous sensory capacity, he absorbed the Zeitgeist and reinvented himself practically every decade—but without ever denying the past. It was an approach deeply rooted in classical maxims that allowed him such transformations: Ponti was not much interested in establishing a principle and then either sticking to it or rejecting it; rather he plumbed the depths of phenomena by experimenting continuously and penetrating them, in this way creating a balance between complexity and simplicity, tension and calmness, lightness and weight, past and future.

The classical was Ponti's yardstick, as it were his balancing pole, in his approach to the Modern. It provides a basic structure that pervades Ponti's work in a non-program-

House at Via Randaccio, Milan, 1925

matic way. He paid closest attention to the creative act, the moment when equilibrium, harmony, clarity, and beauty are achieved. He knew that progress, in the end, could only be achieved in small steps. His artistic demand for perfection, expressed for example in his striving for the "finite form", was combined with his intuition in taking compositional and formal decisions that are both original and difficult to apprehend. Thus Lisa Licitra Ponti recently characterised him in *Domus* as follows: "Ponti is a modern case of the antique architect".

Ponti maintained a non-dogmatic relationship with the Modern: in favour of the Modern, he used to compare the residential building to a car, asking the question, why do people, when it comes to transport, insist on the latest thing in technological discovery but content themselves with the prospect of living in obsolete walls? On the other hand, he had no hesitation in saying, for example, of functionalism that it would force architecture into the straitjacket of time: "Beautiful architecture has lasted beyond its initial aspect, scope, and function, and has often successively served different purposes. The right of an architectonic work—and (...) in the end its right to last as well—is based on its beauty, and not on its function. Because it takes up a new function: Beauty. Beauty is the most resisting material. It opposes itself to destruction by man, who is time's most fierce ally."

Playfulness is an important part of Ponti's architecture. Playfulness characterises his skilled handling of colour that he owed not least to his passion for painting. His relations with his materials were also playful, never setting his eye on "first choice"— on the contrary, he used to search the backrooms of his suppliers' workshops to hunt for the most knotty and peculiar piece of wood, or the most natural marble. He let valuable marble be cut against its veins, creating in this way new sorts of marble. He also transformed structural ceramics into surprisingly new forms: he used them as if they were pebbles, smashed them into mosaic pieces, cut them into diamond shapes in order to clad walls, ceilings and floors. Such a playful experimental approach to application can also be found in his frequent use of optical effects, aiming to stage his buildings as phenomena. In this way one can approach Ponti from a phenomenological point of view.

Ponti can be regarded as a personality who promoted in Italy the artistic design of industrial products, just as the *Deutsche Werkbund* (German Association of Craftsmen) had done years earlier. In this way he played a crucial role over decades in shaping the face of Italy and can rightly be seen as one of the fathers of Italian design.

In all this Ponti displayed a high degree of independence that lifted him above the times and enabled him to employ fashions of the day, but also to disregard them. As early as 1933 art critic Edoardo Persico characterised him: "Gio Ponti is a lonely inventor for whom art history doesn't take place in the sense of progress but as a sequence of different phenomena." In this sense Ponti's architecture is not to be viewed as a progressive one, which means that it is not to be understood as a series of creations where the latest one emerges from the previous one, but rather as expression of a process of "endless refractions". Everything he creates has its own individual character and therefore cannot be seen as a stage in his development. Now and then a few older elements from older works are taken over but in most of these cases it is a matter of treatment, resumption and mirroring of a concept. We should record that Ponti was brilliant in the originality of his ideas rather than in systems built up in single and therefore comprehensible developmental steps. That is the reason why, although he was a professor at the Polytechnic in Milan for many years, at no time was there a Ponti school.

Interior view, sketch in watercolours

Gio Ponti was true to himself. His appearance was elegant in the basic etymological sense of the term, meaning he had the competence to choose. The way he dressed himself was well-chosen, and, in his day he was included in the list of the 100 most elegantly dressed Italian men; his everyday clothes, which he designed himself, were stylish, of functional simplicity, with cleverly applied pockets and charmingly crumpled. And charming as well were his avowals to the gentle sex: being a gentleman, an admirer of the feminine, Ponti dedicated to innumerable ladies his innumerable little drawings. His personality was characterised by a great calmness, prudence, and cheerfulness. He did not have an intellectual appearance, but captivated people with his sense of humour, and whoever met him would remember his disarming beaming smile—even his "so-called enemies" (as he used to say, and he cultivated the childish naivety not to notice that he had enemies). With his wife Giulia, Ponti was bound by sincere quarrelsomeness for more than 50 years. One of the main themes of their marriage was the question to whom Ponti was married—to his wife or to architecture. Melodramatic scenes were not rare when Giulia brought about so many cosmic disasters by disturbing the equilibrium of the Pontiesque total work of art by unauthorised acts of interior decoration, such as tidying up, re-arranging the furniture, or positioning an innocent flower pot in the wrong place.

The hospitality of the Pontis was legendary. Representatives not only of the Italian arts and culture but from all over Europe were welcomed in their open house. Ponti's openness and skills as a communicator helped him to take on an influential, almost unique, position within the Italian cultural scene. As one of the most famous Italians of his time, he was afforded almost mythical reverence in his hometown Milan. His versatility and virtually inexhaustible creativity would have secured him a rank among the greats of modern architecture. However, as a result of his independence and his role as a mediator he got caught in the crossfire between the modernists and the

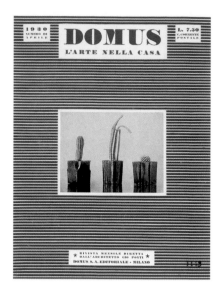

Cover of *Domus*, April 1930

traditionalists, and was threatened with being pushed onto the sidelines. Only recently is a re-evaluation of the man and the work taking place on an international level.

Giovanni 'Gio' Ponti, born in Milan in 1891, came from a good middle-class family. His father Enrico Ponti held a management position at the Edison Company. As a child he already revealed artistic talent and was attracted by painting, and even in old age one of his habits was to present relatives and friends with drawings as a welcome gift. However, obeying the wishes of his parents, who both considered the profession of an architect more solid that that of a painter, he enrolled at the Faculty of Architecture at the Polytechnic in his home town in 1914.

The artistic world of the northern Italian metropolis in those days was under the sway of a futuristic uproar. In 1909 the writer Filippo Tommaso Marinetti, doubtless under the influence of Nietzsche's and Bergson's writings, stepped onto the public stage with his Futurist Manifesto, demanding a fundamental renewal of the arts and radically condemning the forces of the past. He wanted to liberate Italy "from its countless museums, ... libraries and academies of any kind"; he celebrated "the beauty of speed", maintaining that "a roaring car that seems to run on grapeshot is more beautiful than the Victory of Samothrace". Consequently he glorified war as the "the world's only hygiene". The whirlwind with which the Modern in Italy announced itself might have been impetuous, but it rattled the doors of a lethargic, academically paralysed artistic world.

Nothing is known about Ponti's involvement with Futurism during this time. He was engaged with his university studies, which were still rooted in the academic traditions of historicism and eclecticism. Students spent hour after hour copying historical examples. However, as an alert observer of his time, he quite likely participated in the debate, although he would hardly have shared the views of the futurists about the destruction of the remains of the past. Independent as Ponti was, it is characteristic that he was befriended by Marinetti.

Between 1915 and 1919 Ponti interrupted his studies and served as a captain in the Pontonier Corps. He was decorated with the medal of honour and the Military Cross. During this time a kind of awakening must have occurred when he spent nights during lulls in the fighting in villas designed by Andrea Palladio, which had been abandoned at the time. Later he declared that his inclination towards the classical derived from having slept in and perceived those spaces with closed eyes. "Who are daddy's masters?" he used to ask his little daughters; "Serlio, Palladio, Vitruvio," Lisa and Giovanna answered in chorus, is if it were a nursery rhyme.

Ponti's classical approach was further shaped by his intensive contacts with the neo-classical countermovement to Futurism *Novecento*, and his friendship with the painters Giorgio de Chirico, Carlo Carrà and Mario Sironi. The *Novecento* art movement and the architectural current which derived from it were inspired by *Pittura Metafisica* (metaphysical painting) and, indeed, these paintings appear like an anticipation of the buildings of the Novecentinists. Giorgio de Chirico, the originator and major exponent of *Pittura Metafisica*, described it in the following words: "It is the silence and the senseless beauty of matter, which appears metaphysical to me, and of metaphysical character appear to me objects which by purity of colour and exactness of their measurements are the antitypes of all confusion and vagueness." On the one hand, the Novecentinists strived to break through the dead end of traditional eclecticism to arrive at a genuine interpretation of the present (*Novecento* is the Italian term for the

Gio Ponti and Antonio Maraini

20th century). However, at the same time they searched for the eternal laws of art and architecture, which for them lay hidden in the classical tradition. Basic principles of the *Novecento* were *disciplina* (order), *serenita* (serenity), and *compostezza* (decency). The Modern and the traditional were placed in a dialectical tension.

The year 1921 was decisive for Gio Ponti: he finished his studies and married Giulia Vimercati, a member of Milan's local aristocracy. Four children resulted from the marriage: Lisa, Giovanna, Letizia and Giulio. The connection with the daughter of one of Milan's most influential families probably opened doors to local high-bourgeois society, where young Ponti with his witty ideas soon got attention, so that it did not take him long to receive his first commissions. The post-war period, faced with a gap in capacity, was in need of new forms of expression. In the same year Ponti started an architect's office together with Mino Fiocchi and Emilio Lancia, which would last with Fiocchi until 1926, and with Lancia until 1933.

It was in these years that Ponti laid the foundation for his later works when he became eminent as an artist, editor and cultural promoter, and played a crucial role in the debate about the revival of the arts. He was among the supporters of the *Club degli architetti urbanisti* (Urban and Architectural Planners Club). It was in this period that he made the decisive contacts, including entrepreneurs belonging to the ascendant Milanese bourgeoisie, who would become important clients in the future.

At the same time Ponti also began to work in arts and crafts and industrial design. As early as 1919, when still a student, he gained attention with his illustrations of Oscar Wilde for the Modernissima publishing house. In 1923 he took over as artistic director of the renowned porcelain manufacturer Richard-Ginori, a post he held until 1930. With his designs he not only earned the company international prices, but also gave an innovative impetus to the Italian ceramic arts as a whole.

The language of Ponti's early houses can be classified as neo-classical with (increasingly) reduced decoration. The influence of academic architecture is still visible in the façades of the residential building in Via Randaccio in Milan with its obelisks and of the country house *L'Ange Volant* in Garches, but behind these façades are already those modern, functional, practical and liveable interiors that are typical of Ponti.

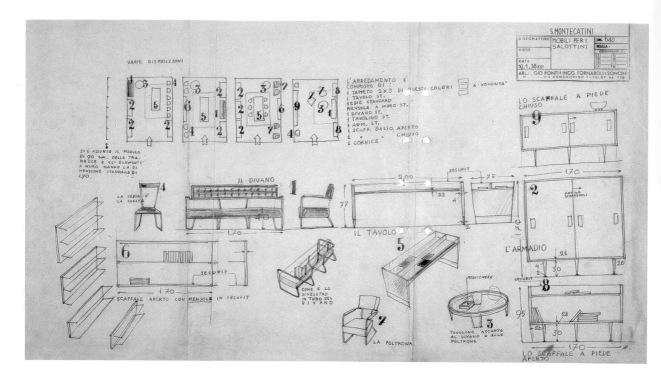

Sketch of furnishings for Montecatini Office Building, 1936–1938

In 1928 Ponti founded *Domus*, a periodical that with its interdisciplinary spectrum covering architecture, arts and crafts, and design was unique in Italian journalism. *Domus* was addressed not exclusively to artists and architects, but tailored to the new class of leading citizens and the broad public with an interest in art. Ponti's aim with *Domus* was to train good taste, to show the reader how to approach his lifestyle decisions with cultivated care and reason—and not least of all to celebrate beauty. However, there was disagreement over the years about the direction of the magazine between Ponti and the publisher Gianni Mazzocchi, whom he had befriended but who nevertheless had in mind, instead, a magazine for the housewife about daily life. Even the number of pages, which Mazzocchi endeavoured to reduce for cost reasons, never seemed enough to Ponti in the face of the wealth of content to be presented. This issue he dealt with from time to time with a typical Ponti trick: some of the pages simply had no page numbers...

Domus also gave Ponti a high-calibre and superior instrument that strengthened his influence on the development of Italian architecture. Not the least remarkable thing—and this was characteristic for an independent spirit like Ponti—was the direction in which the magazine developed. It did not in any way become the mouthpiece of the *Novecento* movement, to which Ponti still was attached during the 1920s. Rather it tended to become much more a forum for the *Architettura Razionale* movement led by Giuseppe Terragni, Giuseppe Pagano, and Carlo Enrico Rava, which had come into being less than a year earlier and, inspired by the *New Building* in Germany and France, was in search of national content and techniques in order to create its own analogous style. Animated by this quest the debate about what might constitute *italianità* and *mediterraneità* in architecture was fought out in *Domus* during the early 1930s. However, beyond this debate *Domus* was a publication of international orien-

Bedroom, ornamentation by Piero Fornasetti
Models designed for the IX Triennial at Milan, 1951

Wooden chair with butterfly pattern
The shape of the back recalls Ponti's famous *Superleggera* chair.

tation in fascist Italy, that presented and discussed modern architecture and its representatives such as Peter Behrens, Ludwig Mies van der Rohe, Erich Mendelsohn, Marcel Breuer and Le Corbusier, even mentioning Soviet Constructivists like Konstantin Melnikov.

The beginning of the 1930s represented a first break for Ponti. During this time several decisive developments took place: Ponti took up his teaching post at the *Politecnico di Milano*, an appointment he would maintain till 1961. And in 1933 he ended his collaboration with Emilio Lancia and began a new working relationship with the engineers Antonio Fornaroli and Eugenio Soncini. This decision marked a fundamental new orientation, and a gradual farewell to neoclassical symbolism. The Ponti-Fornaroli-Soncini office remained in existence until 1945; Ponti would continue to work with Fornaroli until the end of his life.

The 1930s showed Ponti the problem of finding a valid form of expression for the Modern in Italy. He refrained from returning to historical stylistic forms, not least because in his opinion none of them was able to express the essence of the Italic, the *Italianità*. Even if he was reluctant to attribute the merit to himself, in the end it was he who played a crucial role in paving the Italian way towards the Modern. Ponti understood that a genuine Italian contribution to the development of the Modern could only appear if it was based on cultural identity. Already in the preface to the first issue of *Domus* in January 1928 he stated: "An Italian style house is not the padded and fitted shelter of those who have to protect themselves from a rough climate, like the inhabitants beyond the Alps who must look for shelter during many months of the year because of the inclemency of nature. The Italian house is the place we have chosen to enjoy our life in, where we happily possess the beauties given to us for long seasons by our land and our sky."

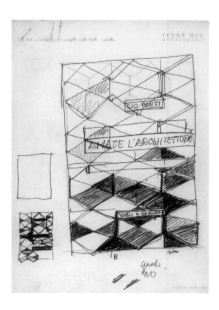

Sketch for the cover of *Amate l'architettura*

Steel knife, fork and spoon, Arthur Krupp Italia, 1950s
The knife features a battered edge, only cutting at its tip; the concave-shaped fork has only short tines in order to make it suitable for sauces.

With this statement Ponti found himself at a great distance from fascist state architecture, first of all from that of Marcello Piacentini with its grim invocation of a glorious past, and indeed Ponti's buildings in their sanguine lightness appear remarkably un-Roman. His spiritual point of reference is Florence, not antique Rome, the Italic, not the Roman Italian. This manifests itself even in buildings like the Faculty of Mathematics in Rome, where, given its function as the seat of a scientific discipline, a certain strictness was predetermined. Indeed, the building is one of the most functional Ponti ever created as is clearly shown by his making the interior of the building detectable on the façades.

Typical examples of a modern Italian domestic culture were Ponti's houses in Milan, which he baptised with Latin names such as *Domus Julia*, *Domus Aurelia*, and *Domus Serena*. For all their modernity, however, they are equipped with large rooms and halls of double height, because "a person wants to have at least in some rooms in his house with a distance to the wall of at least six or seven yards from where he is standing, and if possible, some ceilings running at least five yards above him". The year 1934 marked the actual beginning of his critical examination of the theme of Mediterraneity. It becomes tangible with Ponti's study of the Pompeian Villa, in which the idea of a central courtyard played a supporting role (which would find its realisation in the villas Arreaza in Caracas and Nemazee in Teheran). The villas Marchesano and Donegani in Liguria were also indebted to the theme of Mediterraneity, where Ponti strived to demonstrate how architecture could contribute to beautifying the landscape.

In 1933 Ponti was the organiser, together with Giuseppe Pagano, of the Triennial in Milan. Inspired by the *Deutsche Werkbund* and the *Wiener Werkstätte* he endeavoured to reconcile the applied arts and industry and to foster cooperation in order to create high-grade arts and crafts products; in this way he became the obstetrician of Italian industrial design. "Industry has style," he wrote, inviting young artists to dedicate themselves to applied art. At a moment when foreign housing and furniture industries posed significant competition, Ponti exhorted the Italians to launch their own modern production effort in which the unique artistry of local know-how was preserved. In this context he established several competitions, projects, and awards, among them the famous *Compasso d'Oro ADI*.

Ponti himself made designs for the glass industry, for the houses of Fontana, Artemide and Venini. For Chirstofle he created silverwork. Additionally he made several thousand designs for chairs, tables, sofas, furniture, and sanitary facilities for enterprises like Cassina, Frau, Ideal Standard and Walter Ponti. He also designed crockery, cutlery (for Reed and Burton), table cloths, curtains and materials, costumes for theatrical plays at the Triennial or the Scala of Milan, sewing machines (in 1948 the prototype of the *Borletti* and, in 1949, the *Visetta*)—and in 1949 an espresso machine with the name *La Cornuta* (horned) for the La Pavoni company. In 1953 he even designed the bodywork for a new car with the name *Diamante*. A great many of his designs also came from the commissions of international companies, among them Krupp, Altamira, Singer & Sons, Nordiska Kompaniet, and Knoll. In this way his work contributed crucially to the spreading of Italian design all over the world.

The 1940s brought some changes in Ponti's editorial activities. As an author, draughtsman, and designer he had, since 1939, contributed to *Aria d'Italia*, a new periodical for Italian art and literature whose editor, Mrs. Daria Guarnati, was one of his friends. His involvement with this lively and innovative magazine may have shown him how far his ideas for *Domus* differed from those of its publisher Mazzocchi. In 1941

Cover of *Amate l'architettura*

Coffee maker *La Cornuta*, 1949

Ponti resigned from managing *Domus* and took over as director of the art magazine *Lo Stile*, published by Aldo Garzanti. In doing so Ponti created an experiment, which, due to difficulties at the time, was not meant to be a long-lasting one: like the French magazines *Verve* and *Minotaure*, the periodical was thought of as a forum for all kinds of artists to exchange their views with each other. In 1947 Ponti and Mazzocchi came to an agreement, and Ponti again took on management of *Domus*.

During the 1950s Ponti and Fornaroli started their collaboration with young Alberto Rosselli. The bulk of Ponti's most important works emerged from this office. It was in those years that Ponti's success reached its zenith and when he celebrated his breakthrough to international status with important public commissions such as that for the Iraqi government to contribute to a project for the urban renewal of Baghdad, where he was in the company of architects such as Frank Lloyd Wright, Alvar Aalto, Le Corbusier, and Walter Gropius. He also realised some government buildings for the new Pakistan capital Islamabad.

In the post-war years Ponti began his examination of what he would call "finite form" (*forma finita*). A formal motive was offered for the unauthorised structural alteration of his first Montecatini office building. This elegant building with its massive volume, where Ponti, following the functionalist principle, only marginally differentiated between foundation, body, and termination, had suffered damage during an air raid in World War II. With its reconstruction commissioner Guido Donegani heightened the building by one floor, thus changing its proportions. He justified these measures by referring to the pure functionality of the architecture. In order to prevent such interference in the future, Ponti began his search for the 'perfect' shape that would exclude any change to the body of the building: "A structure made of a pure repetition of elements without ratios that establish unchangeable limits cannot be an architectural work of art because it is not a form and therefore not something 'finite' (a form that is not finite in itself does not exist). Such a structure is merely a building at best only a rhythm, not music; only a fragment, not a finished work. ... An architectural work of art is something 'finite' that cannot be changed in any way. Pisa's Baptistery cannot be made taller, a painting cannot be enlarged, a piece of music cannot be lengthened."

Ponti found the 'perfect' shape in the symbol of the crystal, which seemed to be an excellent example for his ideal building: "Pure architecture is a crystal. When it is pure, it is clear like a crystal—magic, closed, exclusive, autonomous, unsullied, absolute, conclusive like a crystal. That can be a cube, a rectangular block, a pyramid, an obelisk, and a tower—finite standing shapes. Architecture refuses unfinished shapes (an endless shape like the sphere will never be architecture; it rolls but it doesn't stand; it doesn't know both beginning and end). Architecture begins and ends. Architecture stands." With the second Montecatini office building Ponti created such a definite shape. However, the perfect expression of the *forma finita* is represented in the body of the Pirelli Tower, where nothing can be added or taken away.

The first Montecatini office building was also Ponti's first skeleton construction. With this method of construction he realised that the traditional subdivision of the façade into wall and window openings was now obsolete, leaving the windows just as openings. Ponti reacted to this abandoning of the staunchness of the walls by laying thin, diaphragm-like sheeting over the openings, avoiding any projection of facework cladding, be it be windows or stone revetment, and by doing so he gave the building volume, noticeable as massive architecture. From such a definition of the façade as

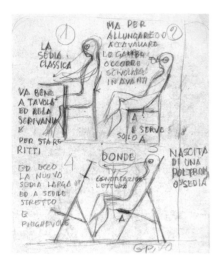

Sketches for "Gabriela, chair with a small seat", 1971

Department store Bijenkorf, Eindhoven, The Netherlands, 1967–1969

surface without supporting function, only changing between appearing opaque or transparent, it was only a small step to the glassed façade, a path many of Ponti's contemporaries chose. But Ponti strived for a livening up of the building skin, and one of his big themes from the 1950s to 1970s was making the façade vivid. He contrived to do this in manifold ways, for example indicating exterior walls as non-supporting by the use of a refined pelmet lighting, thus emphasising its lightness, or cladding the façades of many of his buildings with diamond tiles to break up the light, or—for example at the Shui-Hing department store in Singapore—colouring them differently, or—as he did at the Bijenkorf department store in Eindhoven—structuring them rhythmically with seams and openings.

Another of Ponti's strategies was exposing the ongoing life of the building on its surface: "The façades of the building, ideally, are intact surfaces, like sheets of white paper. The mysterious game of architecture—the design, the life—starts with the windows. The tomb has no windows in its façade because nobody will ever come out of it. A window means life—the interior." In this context Ponti developed the "furnished window", defining it as follows: "An interior room normally has four walls. A room, however, of which one of its walls is a glass front, has only three walls and an opening." By giving such an opening stability and depth with a furniture-like framework composition, he could now say: "A room with a 'furnished window', however, has again four walls of which one is transparent."

The "furnished window" was realised in his own house at Via Dezza, where Ponti would live until the end of his life. Here he also created his own version of a free ground plan that, also a child of the modern skeleton structure, came to maturity in the mid-1950s. He refined these ideas with the villas in Venezuela and Iran, where he created complex interior landscapes with atriums, galleries and pedestals.

In the field of furniture design Ponti arrived at solutions that made history, for example with his famous chair *Superleggera* (Super light) which, developed in the

The *Gabriela* chair, 1971

1950s, is still produced today. With this chair Ponti wanted to make a piece of furniture that is solid and light at the same time. The innovative chair *Gabriela* was created as a result of an analysis of the human sitting posture. Special features of this chair are the extensive back and the small upholstered seat.

In 1957 Ponti left a legacy to the world with his book *Amate l'architettura*. It does indeed provide a key to his view of himself. This collection of texts in his typical kaleidoscope-like manner can be seen as an introduction to various aspects of architecture. These texts appear like individual diamonds, timeless facts, whose relation to each other the reader is required to find out by himself. Ponti himself undertook the layout of the book: individually coloured paper for each chapter, on its cover black and green hexagons on a white background, and the imprinted motto: "Architecture is a Crystal". Layout, title, and content form an intrinsic whole. The book is like a microcosm of Ponti's work.

The idea of the crystalline shape, manifested in the shape of the diamond, and, derivatively, the hexagon became in the following years the principal motive in Ponti's work, from the iconography of the Pirelli Tower to the shaping of the windows of the San Carlo chapel, or the façade of San Francesco in Fopponino, and from there to the diamond-shaped tiles of the villas in Caracas and Teheran, or of the Denver Museum.

The crystal is also connected with the dematerialisation of the exterior walls, which found its culmination in the sail-shaped tower of the cathedral in Taranto. With its hexagonal openings the architecture seems to dissolve into the sky. Embedded in a mighty axis the building arises like a heavenly manifestation before the observer's eyes. The impression of dematerialisation is strengthened by the reflection of the building in the water in front of the building. This effect can also be seen as a manifestation of the idea that, in the end, existence is solely revealed in appearances.

1923–1930 ▸ Porcelain Designs for Richard-Ginori Company

Top row left to right:
China Plate *Piatella*, *Vase with Women, Flowers and Architecture*, 1925; Majolica Vase *Prospettica*

Below:
Design sketch for a plate

Opposite Page:
***Conversazione classica*, China Vessel with a Lid, height 57 cm**

Ponti's contribution to the applied arts began with his work with ceramics manufacturer Richard-Ginori, a company that emerged from the amalgamation of two large ceramic manufacturers based in Milan and Florence. In 1923 Ponti took on artistic management of the company, immediately proving his commitment in this field by participating in the first international exhibition for arts and crafts in Monza. The year 1925 brought initial international success: Richard-Ginori won the *grand prix* at the Paris "Exposition des art décoratifs et industriels modernes".

Ponti completely changed the production process at Richard-Ginori. He invented new product lines and merged the existing ones into families in order to apply serial production methods to individually manufactured arts and crafts objects. He created the *Grandi Pezzi d'Arte Destinati alle Collezioni e ai Musei* collection (large objects for collectors and museums), which included *La Conversazione classica* (Classical Conversation), the majolica vases *La Casa degli Efebi* (The House of The Ephebes), and *Prospettica* (Perspective). He searched the company's archives for old, never-used designs, imbuing them with a contemporary style through his own colourful personal touch. He also contributed to the promotion of the Richard-Ginori brand, creating the first sales catalogue of items and personally devising the advertising campaign.

The time with Richard-Ginori was of fundamental importance for Ponti's career, including his future role as an architect. This was his first creative encounter with materials he would often use in his later work. He not only valued the lustre and purity of porcelain but also discovered qualities such as its plasticity and ability to defract light through the use of pebbles, or diamond and rough-hewn stones, or small mosaic stones for cladding.

1925–1926 ▸ *L'Ange Volant,*
Country House for Tony H. Bouilhet
Garches, Hautes-de-Seine, France

Main building, garden front
The classical symmetry stands in contrast to the modern design of the windows.

Ponti's first work outside Italy was realised in Garches, a location famous for its experimental architecture, including Le Corbusier's *Villa Stein*. Here Ponti built a country house for the French-Italian family Bouilhet, calling it *L'Ange Volant* (The Flying Angel). Tony H. Bouilhet, a nephew of Ponti's wife, was the owner of the famous French silver manufacturer Christofle, for whom Ponti also prepared some designs.

At Garches, Ponti introduced for the first time his version of an entrance hall, a two-storey hall with a generous stairway, breathing light and air through the whole house. The house also exemplifies Ponti's notion of the clear separation of the house into sections for daytime, nighttime and work.

The decoration of the blue and gold coffers in the ceiling is also by Ponti, as is that for the interior floors of the villa, which include light red linoleum, ceramic tiles, wood, and wall-to-wall carpets.

Right:
The central hall of double height with a stairway to the gallery features a painted ceiling designed by Ponti

Below:
Ground plan of the ground floor and first floor

Bottom:
L'Ange Volant, **the flying angel**
Ornament above the entrance at the back façade

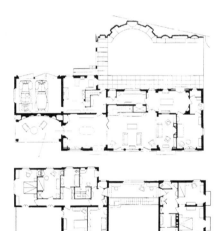

The architect presented in this building his version of a modern classicism, whose simple use of space was convincing internationally, enabling Ponti to promote his *casa all'italiana* abroad as "clear, friendly, hospitable, simultaneously intimate and solitary, with well-measured proportions and manorial style".

1928–1930 ▸ Residential Building at Via Domenichino

Via Domenichino 1-3, Milan

Opposite page:

General view of the corner building
The simplification of the decorative elements indicates the transformation to more modern shapes.

Before Ponti started on this house, he designed his first residential building between 1924 and 1926 at Via Randaccio in Milan. It boasts a concave façade with a curved attic, crowned with a small obelisk. The openwork gable leaves room for a recessed terrace. Compared to this early work, the dwelling at Via Domenichino shows clearly that the architect now aspired to a higher simplicity, abandoning historicising décor in favour of modern forms of expression. The house is striking with its red plaster and impetuous lantern, and also stands out because of its exposed situation at an important street crossing in the newly enlarged exhibition area.

The ground plan, designed by Ponti and his collaborator Emilio Lancia, is L-shaped. The entrance to the building is situated at No. 1 Via Domenichino, the driveway at No. 3. At the entrance, access to the upper floors divides in two: a passage on the right leads to the manorial section of the house, while that on the left leads to the service entrance. The façades of the house are divided into three parts; however, the classical precision of the structure is lightened by the playful diminution of the uppermost floor. The two-storey high base is clad with travertine. The middle part of the building is plastered with red terranova; the flush mounted terraces and the striking turret above the corner give the impression that the building dissolves into the sky.

Floor plan of the ground floor
At the bottom the two entrances: left the main entrance, right the entrance for domestic staff

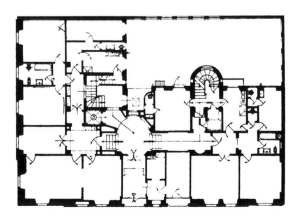

1931–1938 ‣ *Case Tipiche*

1931–1933 Domus Julia, Fausta and Carola, Via Aristide De Togni; 1933–1938 Domus Livia, Serena, Onoria, Aurelia and Flavia, Via Letizia; 1934 Domus Adele, Via Coni Zugna 29; 1935–1938 Domus Alba, Via Carlo Goldoni 63, Milan

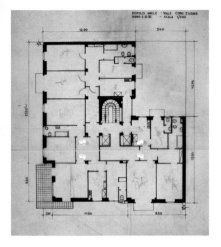 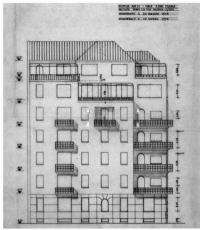 

Domus Adele, Viale Coni Zugna, Milan, 1934
Ground floor plan, lateral view, and historical photograph

Opposite page:
Case Tipiche at Via De Aristide Togni, Milan, 1931–1933
The façades are vertically divided into differently coloured sections: green, red, and yellow.

Below:
A sketch with colour samples

Ponti presented his views on domestic architecture in his book *La Casa all'italiana*, written between 1928 and 1933. Here he portrays modernist principles as an inevitable development. It was precisely these principles that Ponti sought to realise with the *Case Tipiche*. In his view a residential building had to be practical, simple and fresh. Like any automobile it should meet the standards of its time, pushing to their limit all the technological means available for construction and decoration. For Ponti it was in the residential building above all that culture found expression.

The *Case Tipiche*, scattered all over Milan, both detached dwellings and units within larger developments, were based on very different commissions. But all of them bear names including the term "Domus", a reference to the magazine founded and published by Ponti from 1928. All of these houses exemplify Ponti's long-held principles: internally they are clearly divided into spaces for living, working and accommodating domestic staff; they also show a clear layout of rooms with built-in cupboards and furniture integrated into the architecture, granting maximum open space for the residents. Commonly used rooms like entrance halls, stairways and hallways were designed extremely logically with great attention to detail and sometimes executed with luxury materials like marble.

The vivid colouring of the façades is characteristic of the houses: wherever possible Ponti used coloured plaster of red, ochre or even green terranova; when this was impossible he chose vitrified brick and travertine. The façades often give the impression of paintings in which modern and classical elements are playfully arranged. The houses at Via Togni and Via Letizia are notable for being drawn back from the street, leaving space for a landscape strip that could be used as front garden.

1933–1934 ▸ Casa Marmont
Via Gustavo Modena 16, Milan

Interior with high ceiling

Ponti introduced this house in his journal *Domus* together with nine 'commandments' in the spirit of Le Corbusier, a kind of manifesto on architectonic progress. First: The alignment of the house must be carefully planned as each room should receive natural light. Second: Each apartment should have a tripartite division into spaces for service, daytime activities, and sleeping. Third: Every apartment should have either a balcony or a terrace. Fourth: Separate entrances to the service and family areas should be located so they are not mutually visible. Fifth: The basements should be hygienic, bright, airy, and covered in plaster. Sixth: Balconies, terraces and windows should be regarded as part of the living area and equipped with curtains and planting boxes. Seventh: The uppermost floor is to be treated as the most important; it should contain a villa-like apartment with bigger terraces. Eighth: Each apartment should be fitted with as much built-in furniture as possible. Ninth: The stairwell should not be monumental but always sufficiently wide.

The exterior design of the L-shaped Casa Marmont, divided into a seven-storey wing at Piazza Novelli and a lower, five-storey wing at Via Nullo, seems to fulfil these 'commandments', not least through the interplay of the terraces (Casa Marmont boasts 17 terraces and balconies) that Ponti had already put to test at the Casa Rasini in Porta Venezia. Despite the classical division of the façades into footing, middle section and attic, the design of the window openings ensures originality. A partiality for linearity can be discerned in the architect's decision to keep the window openings free of any framing; only a four-inch thick stone window-sill underlines each opening. As he had done in some of the *Case Tipiche*, Ponti arranged and made the façade rhythmical by creating vertical rows of windows: a row of round-arched windows, for example, is flanked by a row of wider, rectangular windows.

Ground plan

Opposite page:
General view

1934 ▸ Faculty of Mathematics Building
Campus of La Sapienza University, Via Cesare de Lollis, Rome

Side view of the lecture hall

Opposite page:
The library with its red and white painted bookshelves

Ground plan

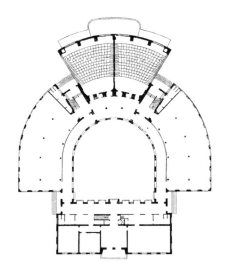

When the architect and urban planner Marcello Piacentini received the commission from Mussolini to build a new university campus (Città Universitaria) in Rome, he succeeded in securing a number of promising young Italian architects for the project. Ponti must have already been held in high esteem since he was assigned one of the most prominent locations, next to the Piacentini's chancellery and opposite Giovanni Michelucci's Institute for Geology and Mineralogy.

The whole undertaking ranks among the most important chapters of Italian architecture in its highly complex engagement with the modern. Clearly at pains to reconcile academic monumentalism with innovative rationalist trends, Piacentini even invited Giuseppe Pagano to collaborate: Pagano was a follower of the rationalist architectural movement MIAR (Movimento Italiano per l'Architettura Razionale), director of the periodical *Casabella* and a clear opponent of Piacentini.

While Ponti never participated in the rationalist architectural exhibitions of the MIAR between 1928 and 1932, he nevertheless delivered here a convincing example of functionalist architecture, characterised by a freedom in design no one else risked. The building has a symmetrical ground plan; its volumetric proportions convey a highly coherent overall appeal. The mathematical faculty consists of two juxtaposed parts: a cuboid structure next to the library entrance that houses the lecturers' offices, and opposite a fan-shaped shell with four lecture halls. Two curved wings, housing drawing rooms, connect the building parts to each other.

The form of the window and door openings is completely in harmony with the function of the rooms. This is exemplified in the big sidelight windows on the smooth outer wall of the lecture halls. At the same time, Ponti did not hold back from leaving his characteristic trademark on the building by using round-arched doors and circular windows: shapes he liked to use very often in those years.

The big window at the travertine-clad entrance façade provides bright light for the library, while highlighting that this is the building's front side. The entrance hall testifies to the great elegance of Ponti's architecture. In front of the diagonally placed panels on each of the side walls clad with white Carrara marble, staggered in juxtaposition and about halfway down the hall, stand two black marble benches. These tricks as well as the extremely original colouring give the hall a lively classicism: the floor and three of the walls are white, the fourth wall is clad with black marble, and the ceiling is plastered in red. The doors on either side have wide round-arched bordering, clad with aluminium panels: a successful experiment in connecting classical form and modern technology. Refined details such as the spiral-shaped handrail or the marble marquetry on the landing put the stamp of the unmistakable style of the Milanese architect on the building.

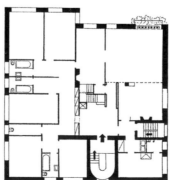
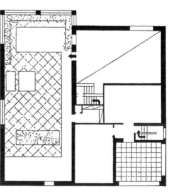

1935–1936 ▸ Casa Laporte
Via Benedetto Brin 12, Milan

Opposite page:
Main façade
Differently shaped openings and protruded canopies in free combination

Opposite page below:
Ground plans of the top floor and the terrace

Below:
The terrace with a small swimming pool, artificial beach, and garden—a very Mediterranean ambience in the middle of the city

Bottom:
Dining hall in Ponti's own apartment
On the wall the family portrait by Massimo Campigle from 1934

Ponti acted on the same principles in building the Casa Laporte as he had with the Casa Marmont. For a few years he and his family lived on the second floor of this house, which contains three apartments altogether. To the earlier programmatic 'commandments' he added two more principles: the layout of the apartments should differ from floor to floor, and each apartment should contain some rooms of double height. This special approach allowed Ponti to experiment with light, space and colour and to create innovative furnishings.

The building rises up to a height of four floors. The façade, facing Via Brin, has an unadorned, rationalist appearance, but is broken down by windows of different shape and size. The progression of the beautiful stairway can be seen from outside through the high vertical window. A small projecting slab covers the entrance and another optically marks off the apartments from the roof terrace. Walls protect the terrace from observation, ensuring uniformity from the outside and intimacy from the inside. As he had done elsewhere, Ponti filled the terrace with roll-out awnings, which also shelter the small swimming pool. The whole impression is of a small piece of the Mediterranean in the midst of Milan.

The mountings of the façade windows are made of stone, standing out only minimally; even the stone slabs of the façade's cladding are fixed with care: the joints are coordinated to alternate with the rows of windows. The foundation, however, shows some irregular special features, providing a free compositional element to the general uniformity of the building's elements.

The building is located in Milan's exhibition district and has been converted into an office building. Some of its original features were lost in the conversion, such as the façade's stone cladding which was replaced by plaster. Nevertheless, Casa Laporte is still one of the most poetical examples of Ponti's architecture.

1936 ▸ Director's Offices of the Società Ferrania
Rome

Presidential desk with intarsia
Tapered legs create lightness.

Below:
Chairs and a wooden divan with slant sash bars

Bottom:
Desk
Oak with glass surface; chair with ferruginous moleskin cover

The fitting Out of the director's Offices of the Società Ferrania in Rome overlapped with a series of similar projects commissioned at that time by cultural and industrial institutions, among them, the design of the Italian cultural institute at the Viennese Palais Fürstenberg and the office rooms of the Vetrocoke Company in Milan. For Società Ferrania he also designed a building with a symmetrical ground plan and rationalist façade at the Corso Matteotti in Milan.

The office of the director Franco Marmont, for whom he had earlier built the Casa Marmont, was decorated throughout by Ponti in horizontal stripes: walls as well as furniture are all covered with black and white striped wooden inlays. The freshness and spontaneity of this uniform black and white look remain remarkably lively and are still praised today by art critics.

In order to maintain the impression of lightness and verticality, the desk's legs are tapered towards the floor, standing in sharp contrast to the mass of the horizontal body of the desk. Here he achieved that "strange equilibrium", the idea for which came to him from Adolf Loos, whom he had known personally: "He used to tell me," he would write in *Amate l'architettura*, "that the foot and the leg of a chair or of any piece of furniture must be always 'a little too thin,' a spire always 'a little too high,' a bridge 'a little too tense.'" Here Ponti is also expressing his desire to push the boundaries of equilibrium. Architecture (even if only expressed in a piece of furniture) is "an impossible equilibrium that succeeds. It is the exactness of an excess."

1936 ▸ World Fair of the Catholic Press
Cortile della Pigna, Vatican City

View into the central gallery

Below:
Entrance of the exhibition hall

Under the pontificate of Pius XI and in the year that the Italian king was proclaimed emperor of Ethiopia, Ponti was commissioned to design the building for the World Fair of the Catholic Press. It was a 'momentous' event, as Ponti himself noted in number 104 of his magazine *Domus*, for here the modern art community was offered the opportunity to show that it could also master the difficult field of religious art.

"I worked at court," Ponti wrote in 1957 in *Amate l'architettura*. He set about the project without shrinking from the historical surroundings in which it was to be embedded. The arrangement of space took account of the visitor's movements; it made use of the optical axis and gradations of light and darkness. Ponti avoided all the usual characteristics of a trade fair, choosing a solemn, ceremonial language without abandoning colour. For the entrance hall he designed a vivid glass window with the figure of Franz von Sales. The walls in the throne hall maintained a yellow tone; the ceiling was dark brown and contrasted by a white linoleum floor.

Among the characteristic features of the project was the stairway, with its lining of white Carrara marble and sides of differently coloured marble. It was a small personal masterpiece in itself. When the pope expressed his astonishment at climbing a coloured stairway which at the top changed into bright white, Ponti answered: "Your Holiness, we architects sometimes perform miracles as well".

1936–1938 ▸ First Montecatini Office Building
Via della Moscova / Via Filippo Turati, Milan

Interior view of an open office

Opposite page:
The H-shaped main building

Desk chair, made by the Parma Company after a design by Ponti

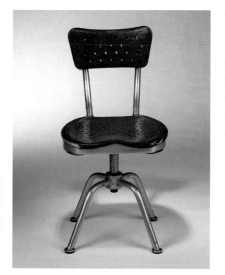

The building Ponti created for the chemicals group Montecatini—his first large office building—offered space for nearly 1,500 workplaces. It consists of three building blocks, arranged in an H-shape. The middle part, housing the executive staff, has an entrance roofed with a free-standing steel and glass construction; the two other wings house the offices for the rest of the staff. In the basement are a number of rooms for after-hours leisure: a recreation room, changing rooms with showers, a library, a hair-dressing salon, a photographic studio, a bar, a pharmacy, a food store, a fashion boutique and a bazaar. The kitchen is separated from the canteen by a glass wall so that guests can watch the chefs at work. The building has sixteen elevators, three freight lifts and a pneumatic tube installation. An air-conditioning system was also installed, an important innovation in Italy at that time.

From the exterior of the building to the smallest detail of the interior fittings, from the aluminium framings of the windows to the ceramic sanitary facilities, from lamps to door handles, the whole project was designed at the Ponti-Fornaroli-Soncini workshops. Ponti proved his ingenious inventive talent in choosing the materials: he cut *Cipollino Rigato* marble against the veins, thus inventing a new sort of marble which he called *Tempesta*.

The façade is marked by long rows of windows, uniform horizontally as well as vertically. Ponti had still not developed his theory of "finite form", which he would implement in with the Second Montecatini Office Building and the Pirelli Tower. Although he was fascinated throughout the project by "non-finite" rhythmical constructions which could be endlessly elongated and heightened, Ponti hesitated to consider such constructions artistic architecture. For him they were rather the work of engineers: as he put it, "Engineering is progressive; by contrast, architecture, an art, isn't". In this sense the Montecatini Office Building is an achievement of engineering; since concept and installation are completely functionally orientated, it numbers among Ponti's works that are closest to rationalism.

After the building's side wings had been damaged during an air raid in World War II, Guido Donegani raised them by another storey, justifying his decision on the basis of the pure functionality of this kind of architecture. Ponti, however, who had designed the building parts on the basis of their volumetric relations, distanced himself from this decision; he drew a lesson from this experience, choosing from then on closed shapes.

1940 ▸ Villa Donegani
Strada Nazionale Aurelia, Bordighera (Liguria)

Above:
Protruded vantage point towards the Mediterranean Sea

Below:
One of the loggias

Opposite page:
North-East view

The client for this villa was Guido Donegani, who was also director of the Montecatini Company, for which Ponti was to build two office buildings in Milan. With this seaside villa, Ponti tried to show his compatriots the possibilities of a Mediterranean architecture.

In the early 1930s, before he committed his own ideas about the matter to paper, Ponti's periodical *Domus* offered a forum for a lively debate about Mediterranean architecture. The debate flared up when some representatives of Italian rationalism, such as *Group 7* led by Giuseppe Pagano, Giuseppe Terragni, and Carlo Enrico Rava, inspired by the style of the *New Building* in Germany and France, strived for national content and techniques in order to create their own distinctive style. In 1931 Rava believed he had found in the "mediterranean spirit" the sources of the *Italianità* that was still missing in the new rationalist architecture. The architectural critic Edoardo Persico, on the other hand, accused Italian rationalism of meaninglessness in his 1934 article *Punto e capo per l'architettura*.

In the same year Gio Ponti formulated his concept of the *Casa Pompeiana*, which can be understood as the beginning of his own examination of Mediterranean-ness. Through Villa Marchesano in 1938, Ponti finally offered his first realisation of this idea. However, his actual contribution to the debate was Villa Donegani, where he demonstrated in an exemplary fashion how architecture could contribute to the beauty of the landscape. "Each house we build on our coasts must make it more beautiful, more enchanting, more inviting and charming," he wrote in 1941 in *Lo Stile*. Only someone who is really familiar with the sun, the sea, the sky, the vegetation and the people of a place can create an architecture that fits immediately into the landscape.

Villa Donegani has an L-shaped ground plan, whose long side faces the sea. The living rooms with a view to the sea are also clearly separated from bed and utility rooms, which are situated at the back part of the house. Three rooms of this house are especially characteristic: the grand salon with its double height, opening to the sea with an extensive window; the loggias at each end of the building; and finally a two-storey open patio, interrupted by a one-storey high dining room whose roof boasts a sun deck. Where the glass front of the dining room cannot be opened a spray system has been installed in order to clean the windows. All walls are plastered with shining white rough Terranova. The awnings are made of strong blue hemp, the furnishings of the solarium and the majolica tiles of the floor are blue and white.

1947–1951 ▸ Second Montecatini Office Building
Via Filippo Turati / Largo Guido Donegani, Milan

Opposite page:
View of the concave façade

Only a few yards away from the First Montecatini Office Building, but built 15 years later, Ponti's second office building rises from a trapezoid-shaped plot of land.

These circumstances prompted Ponti to comment on the relationship between architecture and the city. He stated in *Amate l'architettura* that the shape and size of new buildings are always determined by two facts: the shape of the land and building regulations. With such major limitations, Ponti wrote, an architect in Italian cities can

Common room, separated by glass dwarf partition walls

Below:
Brightness and space are features of the rooms.

hardly do more than design the façade, having neither any influence on the alignment of the building nor the ability to create an architectonic work of art in the purest sense.

Despite these limitations, Ponti succeeded in creating with the Second Montecatini Office Building a modern, diversified building that offers different views from all sides to create an always changing spectacle. Walking along the building with a view to the concave façade, the viewer's impression changes: from the front the façade seems to consist completely of glass, but from the side, viewed from an oblique angle, a surface of pure aluminium appears.

Perspective of the dancing hall
The function rooms feature parquet floors and modern furnishings.

Opposite page:
Interior view of a cabin with functional furnishings

Below:
Interior design of a dining hall
The walls are decorated with paintings.

In the 1930s Ponti displayed the interior design of a luxury cabin for a transatlantic passenger liner at the fourth Monza triennial. After the end of World War II, when the ships of the Italian fleet were renovated to again serve transatlantic routes, Ponti began to develop ideas for an Italian style of ship design. He took part in the renovations of the sister ships *Conte Grande* and *Conte Biancamano*, of the *Andrea Doria* and the *Giulio Cesare* and of the *Oceania* and *Africa*. In his periodical *Domus* Ponti tried to convince experts as well as passengers that ships were not only a means of transport but also artistic manifestos for a nation. For this reason he took care not only in designing furniture and equipment but also in equipping the ships with contemporary works of art as an expression of Italian modernity and culture.

During the work on the *Conte Grande* and the *Conte Biancamano*, Ponti cooperated with Nino Zoncada. On the *Conte Grande* the interior fittings were completely renewed; on the *Conte Biancamo*, in cooperation with other architects, some rooms were newly furnished.

Interior design of the salon of the *Conte Grande*, 1950
On the wall a large inlay work on golden ground with the symbolic depiction of the four seasons, on the ceiling a pattern of shining stripes

Banquet hall of the *Andrea Doria*, 1952
Partial view of the ceiling area lighting

On the *Conte Grande* the first-class rooms were joined without interruption. Wide openings or glass windows offered a view from the hall into the ballroom. Prefiguring many later interior designs for ships, pale gold anodised aluminium was used here for the first time, giving the rooms their unique appearance. In the ballroom vertically grooved aluminium plates were used to create a seamless surface throughout. To reduce the optical impact of the very bulky supporting columns, Ponti created an aluminium cladding tapered towards the top. The 'shining' ceilings (partly luminescent, partly light diffusing ceilings) contributed to the lightness of the room design.

Smooth aluminium lining served as balustrades for the stairs, emphasising and enlivening the course of the stairway. The cladding of the wide stairway in the hall was also made of aluminium, flanked by two ceramic caryatides by Fausto Melotti; at the top of the stairway hangs the *Allegory of the Passenger*, a large verre églomisé painting, not only designed but also executed by Ponti, together with Edina Altara. One of the salon walls is completely taken up with a painting by Paolo de Poli. Executed in enamel on embossed copper it represents four boats, symbols of the four seasons.

Salon of the *Conte Biancamano*, 1950
By the use of ceiling light, paintings on all walls
and modern furnishing, Ponti lends weight to the
specifically Italian style of the ships.

Right below:
Sketches for the *Conte Biancamano*, 1950
Section and ground floor plan of the dancing hall

Below:
A cabin on board the *Andrea Doria*, 1952
Decoration with zodiac signs

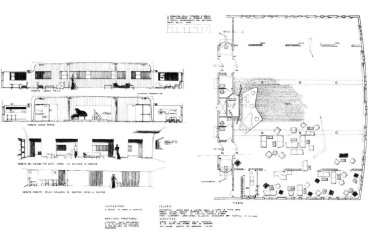

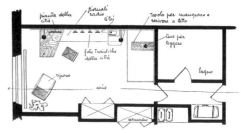

1951 ▸ Hotel Room for the IX Milan Triennial
Milan

Opposite page above:
Interior of a hotel room with functional panel

Opposite page below:
Ground Plan
Ponti made the most of the available space.

Wardrobe side of the hotel room
The wall of mirrors reflects the light and optically enlarges the room. The bookstand can be folded into the wall when not in use.

Gio Ponti used to travel a lot, but he never really left home. That's how his daughter Lisa portrayed him in her book *Gio Ponti – The Complete Work*. On long plane trips he liked to write letters to his co-workers, and he used to draw in cars, even when he was behind the wheel. He expected a hotel room to be comfortable and practical. However, he often observed that they were badly laid out and sloppily furnished, cluttered up with furniture wasting precious space. In protest against this state of affairs, he had already presented suggestions for improvement to the tourism section of the seventh Milan triennial. For the ninth triennial in 1951 he designed the prototype of a hotel room with the measurements of 13 x 10 feet.

Almost all functional elements in this room are situated in the corner panels that run along two walls—a principle Ponti had worked with since the 1940s. The panel also serves at the frame for the bed. Located here are fixtures for a small folding table for breakfast in bed, as well as a reading lamp, radio, cigarette lighter, ashtray, remote control for all electrical devices, telephone, magazine rack and bookshelf, and photos and town map. All furniture is covered with sun-yellow melamine; Ponti also used the colours pea-green, Pompeian red and blue. For the floor he chose a rubber covering by Pirelli in *Giallo Fantastico* (fantastic yellow).

1951–1955 ▸ Residential Quarter Harrar-Dessiè for INA-Casa
Via Harar / Via Dessiè / Via Novara, Milan ▸ with Luigi Figini and Gino Polloni

Sketch of the master plan

Opposite page:
Apartment building in white and ochre
The hexagonal recesses and the colouring convey the impression of modern comfort.

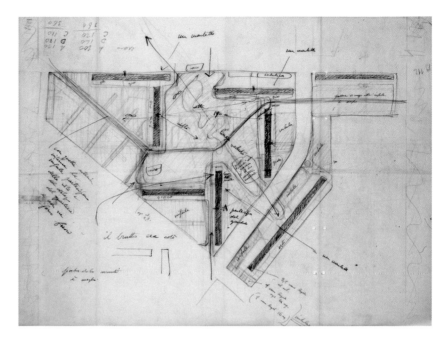

Red apartment building
The maisonettes at both ends of the uppermost floors give the façade a characteristic look.

In 1951 Gio Ponti, Luigi Figini and Gino Pollini won the commission for the master plan for government-supported domestic construction in a new residential quarter of the INA-Casa.

It was not the first time that Ponti had taken on an urban planning project. As early as 1927 he participated, together with the *Club degli Urbanisti* (association of urban planners), in the competition for the Piano Regolatore Generale di Milano (general development plan for the City of Milan), and in 1936, together with Giuseppe Vaccaro and Enrico Del Debbio, he designed the master plan for Addis Abeba in Ethiopia. He also participated in renewal of the former goods yard of the railways Scalo Sempione in Milan, realised the INA building in Via Manin, and, finally, in 1948 contributed to the design of the QT8, Quartiere Sperimentale dell'VIII Triennial.

The new residential quarter of the INA on a large triangular terrain consists of multistorey apartment buildings as well as single-family houses. The latter are grouped into *insulae* (islands). Standing out in Ponti's master plan is the large main vein, drawn in yellow. It stands for a street which would run through the entire quarter, making the *insulae* with their ramifications accessible, and linking them to the master plan—however, it was not realised. The master plan shows a flexible development in a parkland setting with visual axes and pathways with a natural appearance between the buildings, running from the centre outwards as well as from one side of the complex to the other.

From Ponti's hand came the design of the first two big houses at the edge of the residential quarter, one red, the other yellow; the red one he designed together with

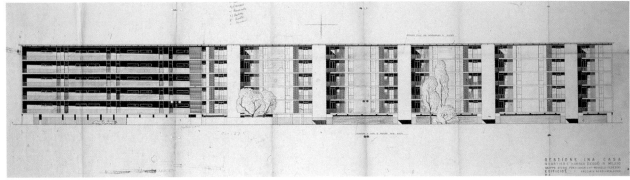

Above:
Historical photo

Below:
Drawing of a front view
This drawing, a joint effort of Ponti, Rosselli, and Tedeschi, shows a coloured design of building E, which, however, was never realised.

Right page above:
Historical photo of the street front
With its upturned roof and the hexagonal loggias on the street side, Ponti gave the building a definite finish in order to prevent later heightening.

Right page below:
Historical photo of the side front

Fornaroli and Rosselli, the yellow with Gigi Gho. The former is interesting because of the duplex apartments on the top storey, giving the building a definite formal termination that cannot be enlarged at will. The red façade lends the building a vivid appearance and stands in eye-catching contrast to the usual grey tones of most of the INA buildings at that time. The second house, in ochre-yellow, white and grey, is distinctive in that the apartments are accessible from exterior corridors. The ground plan clearly shows Ponti's partiality for the hexagon that he developed at this time, even in the projecting exterior corridors at the back of the building that stand out through an oblique bordering façade. The shape of the roof, inclining at the narrow sides of the house, attests to the idea of "finite form".

Despite being limited to simple materials and modest financial means, Ponti did not restrain himself in the use of shapes and colours. This was not a matter of expressing his personal style, but more about the modernity and culture of these so-called "everyman's dwellings".

1952 ▸ Studio Ponti-Fornaroli-Rosselli
Via Giuseppe Dezza 49, Milan

Opposite page:
The central hallway with the drawing desks on the left

Right:
The garden side of the workshop
Next to the lawn, used for relaxation purposes, the drawing tables used to be put up in the open air.

Lisa Ponti and Enrichetta Ritter in the editing office of Domus
Parts of the workshop were reserved for the editing of the periodical.

In 1952 Ponti and Antonio Fornaroli took Alberto Rosselli, Ponti's son-in-law, into their office. Together they moved into a former garage of 7265 square feet, which they had transformed into a workshop. This "Barn", as Ponti would call it for the rest of his life, was an extremely unusual working space, where the designers could even drive in with their Vespas and park next to their drawing equipment. With this space Ponti realised his dream of cooperation among different artistic disciplines under one roof. Conceptually the "Barn" was a manifestation of Ponti's approach towards the total work of art: it was a factory for ideas where Ponti went from desk to desk, giving advice, as in an acrobatic "graphic-verbal ballet", as Ico Parisi once described it. But it was also a place for family celebrations.

The interior space, a large office of 50 by 150 feet covered by a barrel-vaulted roof, was divided into four zones: studio, editorial department for the periodical *Domus*, school and gallery. In the gallery furniture, ceramics, textiles and glass works were exhibited by turn; the school was conceived as a workshop for students and young artists. The whole "Barn" served at the same time as an exhibition place for different materials: the floor in the studio-zone was covered with different types of linoleum and rubber matting, while the zone for furniture exhibitions was laid out with marble slabs of different shapes and colours. The space was simply divided by different kinds of Venetian blinds and partition screens, depending on whether the materials used were opaque or transparent, smooth or wavy, colourful or pale. Outside the "Barn" was a garden, which was subdivided as well: there was a section equipped with marble tables where the staff would work in the open air, while another section was covered with plants and used for recreation.

1952–1958 · Carlo Maurilio Lerici Cultural Institute

Gärdesgatan 14, Stockholm, Sweden ▸ with Pier Luigi Nervi and Ture Wennerholm

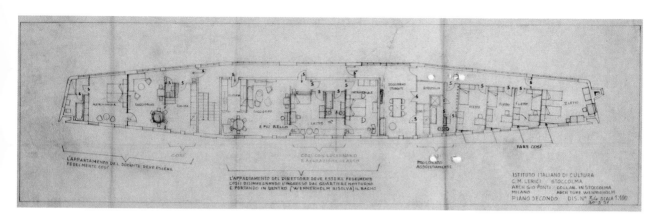

Ground plan of the second floor with furniture, 1957
Ponti drew up the apartments of the lecturers and the institute's director with precise instructions for the architect Wennerholm, who was entrusted with the technical realisation.

Opposite page:
View of the link between the two wings of the building

Interior view

Situated at the edge of the Ladugards-Gärdet, the building consists of two parts, a narrow, long part decorated with white mosaic paving stones, and a low, stubby building, clad with ochre ceramics. The building's interior is surprisingly bright owing to the floor made of white Carrara marble that reflects the light from the window front to the garden and the round skylights. The trapezoid conference room can be enlarged or diminished as desired thanks to the translucent large sliding doors that provide a 'dematerialising' effect when looking towards the entrance hall. Between the conference room and entrance hall is a small kitchen that can provide guests with refreshments at any time.

The hall for cultural events, film screenings and the like has seating for 85 visitors. The reinforced concrete ceiling with its honeycomb structure is a fine example of the collaboration between Ponti and Nervi. The ceiling construction is enriched by the lighting system of backlit ceiling panelling Ponti also used for his ships' interior designs. Ponti also designed the stage curtains with their geometrical decoration in ochre, green and blue. The library receives its light as much from the park through horizontal windows as from the courtyard through vertical windows. The horizontal windows are placed high up in order to provide enough space for bookshelves.

The office rooms running along the hallway in the upper floor are all orientated towards the park. The exhibition hall is in the basement with glass bricks under the ceiling letting in daylight, an arrangement Ponti had already used in the architectural faculty in Milan. The complete furnishings of the cultural institute were designed by Ponti, from the *Round* armchairs to a wonderful chest of drawers clad with white melamine and decorated with violet, blue, green, and black inlay work.

Although it is a public building, the institute offers the comfort and homeliness of a villa. Ponti succeeded in creating a jewel with this building, and he was especially pleased when visitors spontaneously praised its "Italian flair".

1952–1957 · Chairs *Leggera* and *Superleggera*

Ponti with two of his *Superleggera*

As early as 1949 Ponti fitted his chairs with vaulted backrests, in order to provide comfortable contact. Simultaneously he made the chair's framework slimmer and pointier in order to lighten it. In this way in 1952 the model *Leggera* (light) was created, delicate but tough. Made by the Cassina workshops, for whom Ponti was to design many other types in coming years, the chair proved to be so strong that it easily withstood the most vertiginous crash tests at the Cassina workshops. It would bounce off but it would never break, it thrills its owner—with these words the creator himself lauded his chair in the periodical *Domus*. The *Leggera*, Ponti continued, meets the standards of any normal chair to the point that it could be seen as the incarnation of the very idea of a chair; the *Leggera* adapts to any ambience, remaining always simple and appropriate. In their endeavours to realise personal style in each small nail, designers increasingly distance themselves from naturalness and spontaneity. The *Leggera*, however, represents the triumph of normality—and the chair would be enormously successful and celebrated as a great novelty.

In 1957 Ponti designed model number 699 and in this way created the *Superleggera*, the super-light chair. The framework boasts a triangular cross section, and the whole chair with its 1.7 kilogram weight is so light that it can easily be lifted by one finger. As if this was not enough, Ponti designed another version that, half black and half white, looks to be even lighter. The *Superleggera* was designated by Ponti also as "chair-chair—without any adjective"; or, even simpler, as a completely normal chair that does not cost much and is indestructible.

Today, fifty years after its invention, the *Superleggera* is still manufactured by the Cassina company, in a version of ash wood, naturally finished or varnished, and with a seating face of Indian cane.

By tapering and pointing the parts, the *Superleggera* (right) arose from the *Leggera* (left).

1956 · Armchair *Round*

The *Round* chair, reduced to its eight component parts

A sample of the chair in white and blue made for the villa Blanca Arreaza in Caracas

It is not easy to select just a few of the vast number of Ponti's chair and furniture designs of all kinds between the 1940s and 1960s to document Ponti's contribution to the worldwide diffusion of Italian design. Ponti produced designs for many international furniture manufacturers, but it was the Cassina di Meda company, run by the heirs of Amedeo Cassina, with which he had a long lasting and fruitful working partnership, leading to famous items of furniture such as the *Distex* armchair, the *Due Foglie* (two leaves) sofa, and the *Lotus*, *Leggera*, and *Superleggera* chairs. One of the most successful pieces of furniture that Ponti designed for Cassina was the *Round* armchair.

The whole armchair is a play of simple geometric shapes, simultaneously connected as well as separated from each other. The *Round* consists of only eight pieces: an upholstered seat and back in the shape of a flat ellipse, sitting on two curved timber girders to which are fixed four metal chair legs with skid-proof feet. The chair attained considerable fame, owing not least to the fact that it was pictured in photos both in its complete form and as parts, demonstrating the simplicity of its construction. Ponti used this chair in many of his foreign projects, each time adapting colouring and material to the ambience. For the Italian cultural institute in Stockholm with its bright colouring, he chose a white-yellow variation, and Villa Arreaza in Venezuela, where blue and white are the dominating colours, was equipped with blue and white *Rounds*.

1953–1960 ▸ Villa Planchart
Caracas, Venezuela

The entrance with roofed parking place

Opposite page:
The living room of double height with a view of the Avila Mountains

Anala and Armando Planchart's aviary
The tropical garden on the south side of the house represents a kind of earthly paradise.

Villa Planchart marks one of the highpoints in Ponti's creativity; it could even be seen as the realisation of his vision for residential buildings. Although striving seriously for modernity and avoiding all traditional Italian examples, Ponti remained indebted to his roots as the "deep and true" tradition. The way he created a villa was felt spontaneously by many to be "Florentine".

With this approach Ponti was following the wishes of his intelligent and broad-minded clients Anala and Armando Planchart. Indeed, he succeeded in realising his ideal of "living smartly". He would later dedicate himself with similar passion and enthusiasm to the other two villas he realised abroad, Villa Arreaza (also in Caracas), and Villa Nemazee in Teheran.

Through Villa Planchart Ponti created, as it were, a gigantic abstract sculpture, where storeys, rooms, views and difference in elevation are intertwined into a "play without interruptions". In 1961 Ponti dedicated no fewer than 40 pages to the house in his periodical *Domus*. Here he explains that the shape of the building is to be regarded from the inside, as it is based on internal lines of sight. He mentions two more compositional principles: the curtain wall and the "self illuminating" architecture. The first

principle is achieved by detaching non-supporting walls from the ground, giving them a hovering appearance and making them, from an aesthetic point of view, lighter. The second principle is expressed by hiding the house's lights behind edges and under the roof: When the night falls and the lights go on, Villa Planchart seem to change into another kind of architecture, with the white and compact shell of the daytime building now appearing with hovering, airy surfaces. In the style of some of Oscar Niemeyer's bold buildings, which had left a deep impression on Ponti, this villa evokes the association of a white butterfly lying on a meadow.

In constructing the house, Ponti took into account both the nature of the terrain and the prevailing direction of the wind; of pre-eminent importance for him, however, were the views, especially the view down into the valley of Caracas. The northern façade, braving the wind, has a concave shape and boasts a wide window-wall with a view down to the city. The convex shaped southern side opens to the tropical garden, an "earthly paradise" where the owners used to grow orchids amidst aviaries with exotic birds.

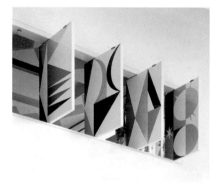

Partial view of the window situation towards the grand patio

As he had with his *Case Tipiche* in Milan, Ponti also created in this house areas for different uses: the northern area on the ground floor is dedicated to the grand salon with its panoramic view, while the southern area houses a kitchen and other service areas. The upper floor houses in its northern section the master bedrooms and guest-rooms, while the southern section is reserved for the rooms of the domestic staff.

In the centre of the house is the patio; it is bordered by the grand salon and a smaller dining room, called *Comedor tropical*. The so-called *Comedor grande*, however, is the stately dining room with its double height and view of the city. The rhythm of the rooms on the first floor is defined by three wide passages leading to the patio, the grand

View of the living room towards the grand patio

Ground plan of the ground floor with sight lines sketched in

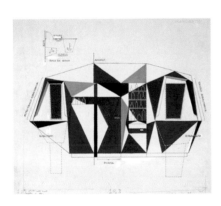

The wall of the bar in the gambling room

salon and the *Comedor grande*. For the master sleeping area, Ponti created two separate but connected rooms. The guest area opens to the patio and is equipped with a gallery, allowing a view down to grand salon as well as to the *Comedor grande*; additionally it has a terrace with northern views and a "nostalgic terrace" facing west. The basement contains further service rooms as well as a hobby-room with a separate entrance.

Giordano Chiesa made most of the furniture following designs by Ponti. The marble originates from Italy, the ceramics on the patio and the statues at the stairwell are by Fausto Melotti, and the facing of the beautiful double fireplace between the stairwell and patio by Romano Rui.

Typical of the creative passion with which Ponti dedicated himself to this total art work are the furniture at the bar corner of the hobby-room with its various fold-out panels, the furnishings of the library, where the owners' hunting trophies could be retracted into the walls, and finally the tiny internal window with its revolving wainscots, decorated by Ponti himself.

1954–1956 ▸ Pirelli Tower

Piazza Duca D'Aosta 1, Milan ▸ with Giuseppe Valtolina and Egidio Dell'Orto

The aerial view shows how the building's body, between neighbouring buildings and the entrance piazza, appears to be pushed up from the depths of the earth.

"She is so beautiful that I'd love to marry her," Ponti told his daughters on the day that "she" was finished. "She" meant the Torre Pirelli. He always spoke about this work in the feminine, and he preferred to call it "la torre" (tower) rather than "Grattacielo" (sky-scraper), and mostly he called the building simply "la Pirelli".

This work marks the zenith of Ponti's career: at the age of 63 he was widely recognised as an architect and contributor to cultural life. The 417-foot high building, one of Milan's landmarks, was one of the first skyscrapers in Europe. Through it post-war Italy presented an impressive testimony to its economic boom.

The high-rise building, first used to house the offices and headquarters of Italian tyre manufacturer Pirelli, was built on the area where the workshops of the same company, destroyed during an air raid in World War II, had once stood. With their plan to erect a prestigious building that would serve as the company's emblem, the Pirelli management first turned to Giuseppe Valtolina and Egidio Dell'Orto, who in turn passed on the major commission to Gio Ponti. Ponti was working with Antonio Fornaroli and Alberto Rosselli at that time, and was joined for the commission by Arturo Danusso and Pier Luigi Nervi.

Bearing in mind the fact that the owner of the First Montecatini Office Building had arbitrarily heightened the building by a floor without regard to the original volumetric relations, Ponti this time—for both the floor plan and building—chose a "finite form", making additions impossible to either the height or the width of the building. By Ponti's side stood Nervi, one of the leading and most influential design engineers of the time, creator of a number of reinforced concrete constructions that were as famous as they were poetic. He helped Ponti by reducing the pressure of the vertical load-bearing structure on both triangular elements at the narrow sides, the inner pillars, and the wind hatches in the central area of the building. This invention became as it were

Right:
Sectional view and ground plan

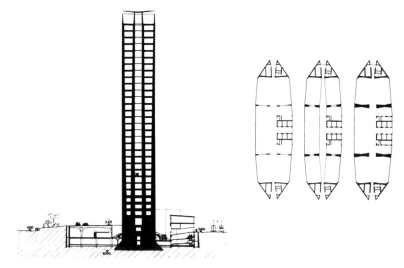

Opposite page:
View from Piazza Duca d'Aosta

the building's graphical motto: the structural framework follows the variation of forces. This is especially evident in the thickness of the pillars that contracts over the height of 31 floors from about 80 inches at the ground level to a thickness of approximately 20 inches at the top, as can be seen from the façade. In order to make this possible Ponti and Nervi searched for any superfluous ballast that could be taken away—this process recalls the creative work of a sculptor, taking away more and more of his creation until it finally reaches the desired "lightness".

Twenty-nine of the 31 floors host open-plan offices. On the top two storeys is the "Belvedere", a roofed panorama terrace, suitable also for special events. For the basement Ponti designed an auditorium.

The government of the Lombardy province has had its seat in the building since 1978. In April 2002 Pirelli Tower made headlines when a light plane hit the 26th and 27th floors of the building, and a repetition of the attacks on the World Trade Center on 11 September 2001 was feared. The damage to the aluminium curtain wall and the ceramic mosaic caused by the crash was relatively quickly repaired, and only two years later the Lombardy government was able to move back into its offices.

The two roofed entrances

Right page above:
The entrance hall
The large window front and the modest furnishings accentuate the floor surfacing of Pirelli rubber in *Giallo Fantastico*.

Right page below:
An open office

63

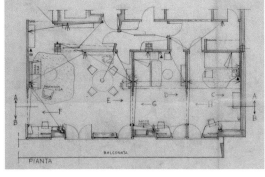

1955–1957 ▸ Residential Building at Via Dezza
Via Giuseppe Dezza 49, Milan

Opposite page above:
The living room in Ponti's apartment
The "furnished window" with its angel figures frames the sky of Milan.

Opposite page below:
Floor plan of Ponti's apartment, 1956

Street front towards Via Dezza
Day and night view to show the optical changing of the protruding and recessed surfaces of the building

Below:
Ponti's apartment, sketch of the wall decoration 1956

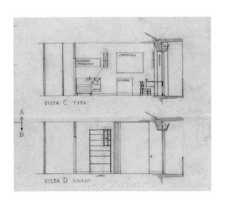

In 1955 Ponti designed for 49 Via Dezza—the very piece of land on which his workshop was already located—a residential building with nine floors. From 1957 until his death in 1979 he and his wife Giulia, along with their two youngest children Letizia and Giulio, lived in the top-floor apartment of the building.

Almost like a manifesto, the building represented all the technical achievements of the 1950s. The façade offered space for individual colouring: the inhabitants of each apartment chose the colour of their floors and balconies themselves so they were able to point out their apartments quickly and easily from outside.

Inside his own flat, pictured many times in *Domus*, Ponti made flexible use of space possible with a floating room division. He refrained from using doors except for the three required by building regulations; he divided the rooms using collapsible partition

Ponti's apartment, view from the living room towards the children's rooms
The folding partition walls enable a view through the whole apartment.

walls; he created indirectly lit furniture, storage walls, and, a special feature, "furnished windows". Through his analyses of space Ponti had been aware for a long time of the phenomen that in a room with four walls, the window wall holds a special status in relation to the others. To take advantage of this fact and to create a direct interaction between the landscape outside and the inhabited rooms inside, Ponti equipped the window wall with consoles, pillar stanchions, and storage places of different heights, thus creating the "furnished window". Towards the end of his life he turned the apart-

ment into his workshop; there he painted angels on perspex and decorated the windows with them.

Ponti's apartment, dining room

1954–1958 ▸ Villa Arreaza
Caracas, Venezuela (demolished)

Opposite page:
View of the living room

The entrance area of the *Diamantina*
The projecting roof, decorated with coloured triangles, stands in contrast to the sumptuous, blue-painted roof overhang with its white border. The walls are clad with white, diamond-shaped ceramic tiles.

Commissioned by Mrs. Blanca Arreaza this villa was the third and last work Ponti created in Caracas. Ponti counted himself fortunate to be the creator of this villa, not least in view of the fact that he succeeded through a modern design in realising to such a degree a deeply sincere and humane architecture.

The *Diamantina*, as the Villa Arreaza was called due to its diamond-shaped ceramic tile cladding, was situated at the new Country Club Quarter amidst the most luxuriant tropical vegetation. In order to accentuate the close connection to nature, Ponti designed a single-storey building with a free ground plan where each room has a view to the landscape or to one of the patios. The lines of vision open in a fan-shape and cross each other thanks to the wide glass doors leading to the garden and to the seemingly endless background of the landscape.

Like the Villa Planchart this building recalls a butterfly, this time in blue; the building appears "like an enormous, light and trembling wing", Ponti wrote in *Domus*. Indeed, it is a very open habitation, the rooms only held together by a thin ceiling-roof spread over the whole building like a huge leaf—or a butterfly's wing. Pondering about the Spanish word "Vivienda" and the Italian expression "un tetto", meaning "a roof over one's head," Ponti came to the following well-formulated definition: "It is the shield under which life happens."

View of the living room

Right:
Dining hall
Ponti designed all the furniture. The material for
the blue and white striped ceramic floor came
from D'Agostino.

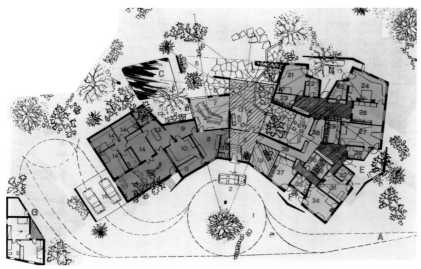

The living room
Everything is in the colours blue and white: floor,
ceiling, furniture and curtains. In the foreground,
vases made of Murano glass by Venini.

Left:
**Ground plan with coloured sectioning of the
specific spheres of function**
From left to right: functional areas, living area,
and bedrooms

1960–1965 ‣ Villa Nemazee
Teheran, Iran

Opposite page:

Living room of double height with the balustrade
The huge window front towards the garden, and the blue and white folding partition wall open the room to the outside. The interior fittings combine furniture designed by Ponti and Persian carpets and art objects.

Exterior view with swimming pool
The southern side of the building with the patio opens towards the garden.

Vida and Shafi Nemazee, the patrons of this villa in Teheran, proved to be as open to Ponti's art as the Plancharts and Blanca Arreaza had before. A friendship developed between the architect and the Nemazees, allowing him to come into close contact with Iran's art and culture.

The ground floor of the villa houses the drawing rooms, opening onto the garden. In the centre is the grand dining hall, leading immediately into the gambling room and further, in a cascade of different perspectives, into the space outside. The upper side of the stairs is clad with white marble with different coloured marble on the front face—an idea Ponti had realized already at the International Exhibition of the Catholic Press. On the upper floor, next to the bedrooms, was a smaller dining room, where the private life of the family took place.

The cladding of the façade with diamond-shaped polished ceramic slabs is modelled after Villa Arreaza. The windows, however, enabling a view from one room into another, are based on Villa Planchart. Apart from these references, Villa Nemazee has its particular individual character, full of compositional surprises. Lisa Licitra Ponti, the master's daughter, recently explained in an essay how the architect plays here with weights and volumes: large and heavy walls, for example, stand in juxtaposition to narrow, filigree mirror-walls. Another play with contrasts can be found in the upper floor where, instead of the floor, the gable roof above the terrace is clad with ceramic cobbles, creating surprising effects. As he did in earlier projects, Ponti engaged his Trentino friend, the sculptor Fausto Melotti. Ponti created in the patio a series of niches and irregular openings for Melotti's sculptures. Inside the building the furnishings designed by Ponti are harmonised with the Persian art works and carpets.

Opposite page:

View of the entrance with canopy

The façade cladding consists of white, diamond-shaped ceramic tiles, made by Joo. The window frames are made of aluminium.

Right:

The patio

The interior façade with its random window openings is decorated with tiles by Fausto Melotti.

Below Right:

Ground plan of the ground floor

Below:

Living room on the first floor

View of the chimney, clad with blue enamelled ceramic tiles and standing on the gallery above the living room on the ground floor.

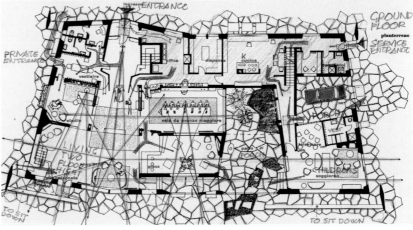

1960–1961 ▸ Hotel Parco dei Principi, Sorrento

Via Rota 1, Sorrento (Province of Naples)

Opposite page:

The walls in the entrance hall decorated with round blue ceramic pebbles

View of the bar
In the foreground the mosaic wall made of ceramic tiles by Joo; in the background the entrance wall with ceramic cladding by Melotti

Some of the thirty different floor tiles used in the rooms

At the beginning of the 1960s Ponti received the commission to design a hotel for the park of Villa Gortchakov in Sorrento on the gulf of Naples. Despite his long-time preference for monochrome concepts—blue for Villa Arreaza and yellow for his own dwelling at Via Dezza—he decided, impressed by the colourful city, on a combination of white and blue.

White and blue—at Sorrento Ponti showed himself almost obsessed by these two colours: white and blue are the table-cloths, the plates and dishes, the bed-linen; white and blue also the walls, the floors, the curtains and the furniture. In *Domus* Ponti raved about the architect's "exhilarating drudgery", describing meticulously the procedure of designing thirty different types of tiles which would be composed to form a hundred differently patterned floors—one for each room. Ponti experimented with new uses for ceramic tiles: for example, by joining Joo's round pebble-shaped tiles into a mosaic. In the entrance hall his friend Fausto Melotti clad pillars and walls with glazed ceramics. The swimming pool in the park looks like a lake; the diving board with its stairs is in the middle of the pool rather than on the side.

Ponti was the creator of a white and blue cosmos—he even went as far as wanting the chefs to serve methyl blue chicken and spaghetti. And although not all of Ponti's wishes and fantasies became reality—and he later complained that he could not express them all—this hotel remains a masterpiece.

1961–1964 ▸ Hotel Parco dei Principi, Rome
Via Saverio Mercadante, Rome

Green and white ceramic mosaics

Partial view of the staircase

The building of the hotel in Sorrento originated only in part from Ponti's hand. With its Roman counterpart he confined himself to a few stylistic measures concerning the design. While in Sorrento the colours white and blue predominated, he now chose the combination white and green. Also in Rome Ponti gave free rein to his passion for ceramics, which found expression not just on the floors in the rooms but also in all the wall and façade claddings. The tiles in the rooms—like those in Sorrento made by the D'Agostino company—have geometric patterns, to which was now added the colour black.

The furniture is made of wood, with inlay work of green melamine; the chairs originate from the Cassina company. The lamps of the Candle company—shining balls set in front of mirrors—are reminiscent of those Ponti used at Villa Nemazee. The dining hall is fitted with large mirrors in order to optically enlarge the room and to reflect the light. To enhance the plump supporting columns in the communal spaces,

Ponti clad them with round ceramic pebbles, or added white pieces of marble and ceramics by Fausto Melotti to the opaque plaster, solving the problem in typical "Pontiesque" manner.

The southern façade with its hexagonal windows is clad with round green tiles (by Joo) on a white background. This was to create surfaces where plants might twine, emphasising the garden character of the southern side.

1961–1964 ▸ San Francesco al Fopponino

Via Paolo Giovio 31, Milan

Opposite page:
Side entrance
The strong jamb of the entrance portal underlines the play with volume. The brown ceramic tiles, used both horizontally and vertically, cause a refraction of the surface.

Among Ponti's ecclesiastical buildings, for example the Camelite-Monastery Sant'Elia at Sanremo (1957–1959), the Milanese church San Luca Evangelista (1959–1961) and the chapel of the San Carlo hospital (1963–1969), the San Francesco al Fopponino church has particular significance both from the point of view of town planning and for its external walls, which seems to dematerialise—a theme Ponti brought to culmination with the cathedral in Taranto.

San Francesco is a complex work whose logic and structure is revealed only to someone who approaches it with great attention. The viewer's eye is caught first by contrasts: between the front façade with its bright diamond ceramic cladding and the lateral façades clad with dark brown ceramic tiles, and between the massive walls and the hexagonal window openings which look as if they have been cut out from a piece of paper and incorporate the sky into the construction. At a closer look contrasts also become apparent between the horizontal effect of the outside and the vertical emphasis of the interior space, as well as between the modern liveliness of the decorative elements and the traditional historical shape of the ground plan. These are only a few of the dialectic elements belonging to the kaleidoscopic fount of Ponti's formal imagination.

"Constructing a church means first of all reconstructing religion in ourselves," Ponti wrote. Indeed, with his design Ponti was striving for the same simplicity and greatness of Saint Francis to whom the church is dedicated. Ponti's idea of connecting the recessed main façade with the lateral wings to create a visual unity transforms the forecourt into a kind of plaza, the external core of the church. The church welcomes the visitor coming from the main road as it were "with open arms"—an expressive gesture with which the church adapts to its surroundings while accentuating itself at the same time. The reference to Saint Francis is also expressed with a garden at the rear end of the building.

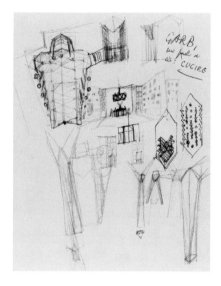

Work sketches

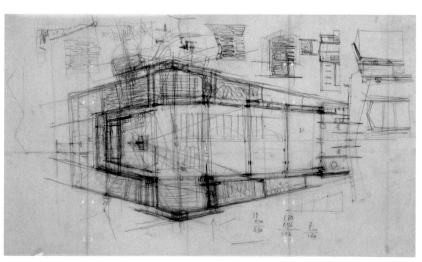

Sketch of the ground floor plan, 1964
The Latin cross is inscribed in the hexagonal.

Opposite page:
Main entrance at Via Giovio

Right:
Interior view

Side façade

Instead of a rose window above the portal, Ponti created a window in the shape of a diamond. Inside the narrow high nave is flanked by two lower nave aisles and partitioned into six bays with supporting ferro-concrete pillars that follow the variation of forces by being tapered towards the bottom. This particular direction of lines as well as the white colour of the pillars, strongly contrasting the dark red of the ceiling, underlines the impression of weightlessness.

Through the vertical window openings with their bevelled edges and pierced sidewalls, the inside of the church appears bathed in a mild radiance. At both ends of the cross aisle is an artistically designed hexagonal window. Looking up to the false choir loft, the visitor's eye is caught by three windows, directing the light towards the periphery walls.

1963–1971 ▸ Montedoria Apartment and Office Building

Via Giovan Battista Pergolesi 25 / Viale Andrea Doria / Via Mauro Macchi, Milan

▸ with Antonio Fornaroli

Opposite page:
Façade towards Via Andrea Doria

View of the lower building part
The random distribution of smooth and diamond-shaped ceramic elements provides playful reflections of the light.

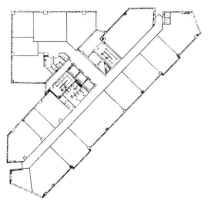

Ground plan of the complex

In this project Ponti had to build within an existing urban context, placing strong constraints on the architect's formal possibilities. The triangular plot alone meant that fundamental consideration had to be given to the hierarchy of street axes. In the first version of the design, Ponti placed a short block running along the main road against a 164-foot high tower situated a little behind it, each of the buildings with its own autonomous articulation of the openings in the façade.

The final version includes, instead of the tower, a longer building complex parallel to the street. Even though the given proportions did not offer him much flexibility, Ponti managed to give the building a rhythmic structure by splitting the surfaces into well-proportioned sections. One by one the jutting panels break down the verticality, bestowing on the building a dynamic expression. The same effect is achieved with the playful placement of divided apertures in the façade in the famous "Pontian" style. At some places—particularly where the ceramic cladding takes on unexpected qualities—such playfulness reveals a work of marvel: through the alternation of smooth and diamond-shaped tiles, the effect is not simply glittering or reflective but also spatial. The contrast between rough and smooth is heightened by placing anodised aluminium window frames level with the façade, the glass surface of the windows combining with the ceramic cladding to form the building's skin, so that the playful dissolution of the massive surfaces of the façade creates that harmonious, airy and light overall impression for which Ponti became so famous.

1964–1971 ▸ Co-Cathedral Gran Madre di Dio

Viale Magna Grecia, Taranto

Opposite page:
Frontal view

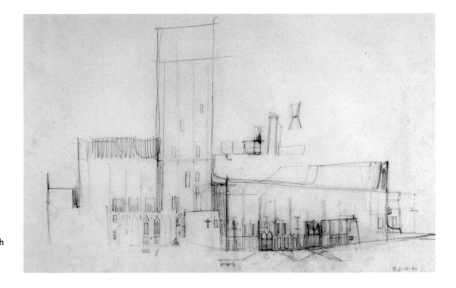

Sketch of the longitudinal section, with which Ponti controlled the proportions of nave and "sails"

In the mid-1960s the city of Taranto decided to provide the new residential quarter of the rapidly growing city with its own house of worship and to complement its venerable historical cathedral San Cataldo with a co-cathedral dedicated to the Great Mother of God (Gran Madre di Dio). The International Institute for Liturgical Arts (IIAAL), to which the archbishop of Taranto, Guglielmo Motulese, turned, commissioned Ponti.

In preparing for the project Ponti intensively examined historical sacred buildings such as the Cathedral and Santa Maria delle Grazie in Milan, San Marco Cathedral in Venice, and St Peter's Basilica in Rome. These cornerstones of sacred art he compared with the romanesque cathedrals of Apulia, such as San Nicola Cathedral in Bari, whose simple elegance impressed him. After a few sketches that he immediately rejected as unsatisfactory, he suddenly realised the necessity in such a building of symbolically connecting heaven and earth, something usually indicated in church buildings by the connection between tower and nave. The low naves symbolise the earth while towers or domes symbolise heaven.

The church Ponti created is rectangular, consisting of a low nave above which, at the spot where the crossing is traditionally situated, an openwork structure rises impetuously heavenward. It is actually a double wall, 134.5 feet high and 72.2 feet wide, with a total surface of 9688 square feet and 80 cut-out rectangular and hexagonal openings, recalling both a tower and a curtain, but most of all a sail. Trying to describe this structure Luigi Moretti turned in *Domus* to phrases such as "irreal meta-matter, a mixture of tangibility and air". Ponti, however, spoke of a "rhythmic series of windows opened towards heaven"; the work would not be finished until climbing plants would took it over, when "nature expropriates it from us and God acquires it".

Side entrance
Clearly standing out is the play with the different volumes of the baptistery, the parish, and the administration building.

Interior view of the church
View from the nave towards the altar

Right page above:
General view of the cathedral with entrance stairway, main façade, and the "sail" above it that replaces the Campanile

Right page below:
Sketch of the side naves with sculptures of the patron saints of Apulia

Unfortunately Ponti's vision did not become reality, and in this sense the building remains unfinished. Today Gran Madre di Dio is besieged by the rank growth of the local building activity but not at all by nature. The garland of white houses on green meadows, which Ponti intended would one day surround the church, was never realised. Instead, tower blocks were erected, giving the place a depressing appearance. The land around the church is in a state of complete neglect. Among the illusionistic effects Ponti proposed only the three-level water pool, reflecting the cathedral, was realised. It at least gives the building some space to breathe.

Inside the church is dominated by the green of the walls and the floor. Sketches from the Ponti archive show that Ponti was only a hair's breadth away from carrying out his vision of decorating the interior with images of the patron saints of all the towns and villages of Apulia as well as with biblical sayings. These plans were not realised. The church was decorated soberly with some metal sculptures designed by Ponti himself.

Gran Madre di Dio represents a kind of legacy left by Ponti. With the church he achieved the dissolution of matter, changing architecture into light. Towards the end of

his life he instructed his daughter: "They say that I reached the apex of my creative life with the Pirelli Tower; but that was in the 1950s. I went on working for another 20 years, and the cathedral in Taranto marks another high point. Please, Lisa, tell this to the people."

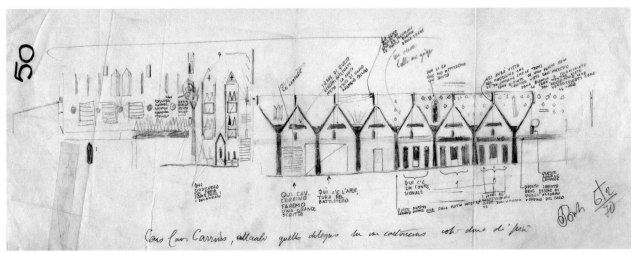

1966–1971 ▸ Denver Art Museum

Denver, Colorado, USA ▸ with James Sudler Associates and Joal Cronenwett

Floor plan of the ground floor

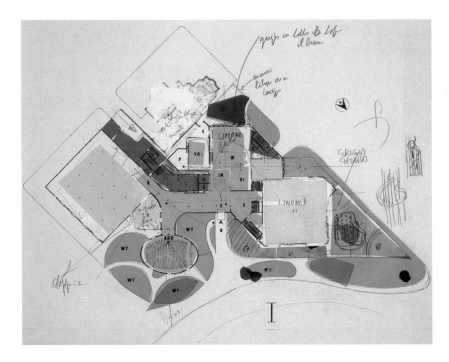

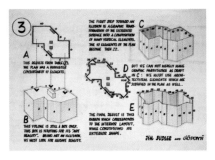

Studies for the development of the building skin

In October 1971 the city of Denver opened the DAM (Denver Art Museum), headed by its visionary director Otto Bach, and boasting one of the most important collection of Indo-American art. It was the first museum building in the United States to house such treasures under one roof.

Compared to buildings of European academic tradition, this museum by Gio Ponti is like a modern fort, where works of art are stored in order to protect them from thieves or devastating storms. The ground plan had already been finalised by the Americans when Ponti was drawn into the project. It was he who helped to give this actually static complex its dynamism and vitality. Supported by the idea that art is in its nature about appearance, Ponti added illusionist elements to the box-like architecture, giving it artistic dignity. The façade sloping steeply upwards results from a vertical projection of the ground plan. Thanks to its countless faceted glass tiles, the façade offers ideal scenery, showing, depending on the light, constantly changing 'compositions'. By revealing tricks that are not always apparent at first glance, Ponti invites the spectator to be present at the "lightscraper-spectacle" produced by the openings in the façade and the reflection of millions of diamond-cut glass stones. "This is the true revelation or the message of this architecture: an invitation to the sun."

Interspersed by numerous loophole-like openings, the originally massive wall becomes lighter and lighter. The openings are not seen as a way to bring light into the building, but rather they offer numerous views: completely unexpectedly the visitor

General view

spots the silhouette of the Rocky Mountains in the distance. In this fashion Ponti completed his quest for the dematerialisation of the external walls, a task he had long worked at and that makes him appear so contemporary even today.

Ponti reminded the critics who reproached him about the considerable amount of money that was spent on the building (six million dollars) of the importance of not losing sight of the value of something just because of its cost. The extension of the building designed by Daniel Libeskind and built between the years 2000 and 2006 doubtless increased this value.

The Denver Art Museum, Ponti's last and most mature building, is a classic example for all those who always want to offset only cost and utility. It is the fulfilment of a dream—the dream of an architect who was able to realise the dream of a client as well as of a whole city: "Nothing was ever created, someone didn't dream of before, and nothing was ever dreamt, that was not realised one day. Dream, citizens of Denver, let's dream!"

Life and Work

Opposite page:

Gio Ponti with Antonio Fornaroli and Emanuele Ponzio watching the model of Pirelli Tower

Gio Ponti with his father

1891 ▸ Giovanni Ponti born 18 November in Milan, son of Enrico Ponti and Giovanna, née Rigone

1914–1921 ▸ Ponti studies architecture at the Polytechnic in Milan, Italy.

1916–1918 ▸ Fights in World War I as a captain in the pioneer corps.

1919 ▸ Illustrations for two Oscar Wilde novels for Casa editrice Modernissima, Milan

1921 ▸ Ponti finishes his architecture studies at the Polytechnic in Milan. Along with Mino Fiocchi and Emilio Lancia he establishes an architect's office. He marries Giulia Vimercati. Participation in the first architectural exhibition of the *Famiglia Artistica*

1922 ▸ Daughter Lisa born

1923 ▸ Artistic director of the manufacturer Richard-Ginori (till 1930). Ponti takes part in the 1st Biennale dell Arti Decorative in Monza. He works on the organising committee for the later Triennials in Monza.

1924 ▸ Daughter Giovanna born

1924–1926
Residential Building at Via Giovanni Randaccio, Milan, Italy

1925 ▸ Richard-Ginori is awarded the Grand Prix at the international exhibition in Paris.

1925–1926
Villa Tony H. Bouilhet, called L'Ange Volant, Garches, France

1926–1933 ▸ Ponti-Lancia workshop

1926–1927 ▸ Along with the *Club degli Urbanisti* Ponti participates in the competition for the extension plan for the city of Milan; the project *Forma Urbis Mediolanum*, to which he contributed, is awarded second prize.

1927
Designs of tin and silverworks for Christofle (Paris), and glass-works for Venini (Murano)

1928–1941 ▸ Founder and editor of the periodical *Domus*

1928–1930
Residential Building at Via Domenichino, Milan, Italy

1930 ▸ Member of the board of directors of the IV Triennial at Monza
Design of the Quattro Pezzi for Fontana and silk-fabrics for Vittorio Ferrari

1931–1933
First Case Tipiche, Milan, Italy: Domus Julia, Domus Fausta, and Domus Carola at Via de Togni

1932 ▸ Daughter Letizia born

1933 ▸ End of the partnership with Emilio Lancia; beginning of collaboration with Antonio Fornaroli and Eugenio Soncini. Member of the board of directors at the V Triennial at Milan
Torre Littoria at Parco di Milano, Milan, Italy (with the engineer Cesare Chiodi)
Design of the Elettrotreno (electric train) Breda ETR 200 (together with Giuseppe Pagano)

1933–1934
Casa Marmont, Milan, Italy

1933–1938
Second series of the Case Tipiche, Milan, Italy: Domus Livia, Domus Serena, Domus Onoria, Domus Aurelia, and Domus Flavia at Via Letizia

1934
Participates at the competition for the Palazzo Littorio at Via dell'Impero, Rome, Italy
Domus Adele, Milan, Italy
Building of the Mathematical Faculty of the University in Rome, Italy

1935–1936
Casa Laporte, Milan, Italy

1935–1938
Domus Alba, Milan, Italy

1936 ▶ Begins teaching at the Polytechnic in Milan. Member of the board of directors of the the VI Triennial in Milan
Implementation of the International Exhibition of the Catholic Press at the Vatican
Several interior design commissions, among them the fitting out of the director's office of the Società Ferrania, Rome, and the Italian cultural institute at the Palais Fuerstenberg, Vienna, Austria
Design for the master-plan for Addis Abeba, Ethiopia (with Giuseppe Vaccaro and Enrico Del Debbio)

1936–1938
First Montecatini Office Building, Milan, Italy

1937 ▶ Son Giulio born

1938
Design for the hotel L'Albergo nel bosco at Capri, Italy (with Bernard Rudofsky)

1939
Takes part in the competition for the Ministry of Foreign Affairs, and in the competition for the Palazzo dell'Acqua e della Luce (Light and Water Palais) at the exhibition E42 in Rome, Italy
Design for the building at Piazza San Babila, Milan, Italy (with De Min, Rimini, Casalis)

1939–1940
Institute for Literary Studies of the University Padua, Italy (frescos by Massimo Campigli)

1940 ▶ Member of the organising committee of the VII Triennial in Milan
Villa Donegani, Bordighera, Italy

1941–1947 ▶ Ponti withdraws temporarily from *Domus* and founds and directs the periodical *Lo Stile.*

1947–1951
Second Montecatini Office Building, Milan, Italy

1948–1979 ▶ Ponti returns to *Domus*, whose editor he remains.

1948–1952
Interior design of the ocean liners Conte Grande, Conte Biancamano, Andrea Doria, Africa Liner, Oceania, *and Giulio Cesare*

1951
Exhibition of the prototype of a hotel room at the IX Triennial in Milan, Italy

1951–1955
Design of the master-plan for the new residential quarter of the INA between Via Harar and Via Dessiè, Milan, Italy (together with Luigi Figini and Gino Pollini). Additionally Ponti erects two buildings for the quarter, one with Antonio Fornaroli and Alberto Rosselli, the other with Gigi Gho.

1952 ▶ Foundation of the Ponti-Fornaroli-Rosselli workshop
Design of the chair Leggera for La Cassina

1952–1958
Italian cultural institute, Stockholm, Sweden (with Pier Luigi Nervi and Ture Wennerholm)

1953–1956
Villa Planchart, Caracas, Venezuela

1954–1956
Pirelli Tower, Milan, Italy (with Giuseppe Valtolina and Egidio Dell'Orto, in cooperation with Arturo Danusio and Pier Luigi Nervi)

1954–1958
Villa Arreaza, Caracas, Venezuela

1955–1957
Residential Building at Via Dezza, Milan, Italy

1955–1961
San Luca Evangelista church, Milan, Italy

1956
Design of the chairs Round and Lotus, also the sofa Due Foglie for La Cassina

1957 ▶ Publishes the manifesto Amate l'architettura in Italy, which is later published in USA (1960), and Japan (1963)
Design of the chair Superleggera for La Cassina

1957–1958
Ministry for Development, Baghdad, Iraq (with Giuseppe Valtolina and Egidio Dell'Orto)

1957–1959
Carmelite Abbey Sant'Elia, Sanremo, Italy

1960–1961
Hotel Parco dei Principi, Sorrento, Italy

1960–1965
Villa Nemazee, Teheran, Iran

1961 ▶ Ponti resigns from his teaching post at the Polytechnic in Milan.
Designs for residential high-rise buildings, Montreal, Canada

1961–1964
San Francesco al Fopponino church, Milan, Italy
Hotel Parco dei Principi, Rome, Italy

1962
Pakistan House, Hotel of the Pakistan members of parliament, Islamabad, Pakistan

1963
Façade of the department store Shui-Hing, Hong Kong
Design for the competition for the Anton Bruckner cultural centre, Linz, Austria (with Costantino Corsini und Giorgio Wiskemann)
Design for the chair Continuum Bonacina

1963–1969
Chapel of Santa Maria Annunciata at the hospital San Carlo Borromeo, Milan, Italy

1963–1971
Montedoria apartment and office building, Milan, Italy

1964
Government building in Islamabad, Pakistan

1964–1971
Co-Cathedral Gran Madre di Dio, Taranto, Italy

1966–1971
Denver Art Museum, Denver, Colorado, USA (with James Sudler and Joal Cronenwett)

1967–1969
Façade of the Bijenkorf department store, Eindhoven, The Netherlands

1968 ▶ Ponti receives an honorary doctorate of the Royal College of Art in London and the gold medal of the French Academy for Architecture.

1975 ▶ Death of Ponti's wife Giulia

1976 ▶ Death of the collaborator Alberto Rosselli. Ponti and Fornaroli continue the work of the studio.

1979 ▶ Gio Ponti dies on 16 September in Milan.

Map Milan

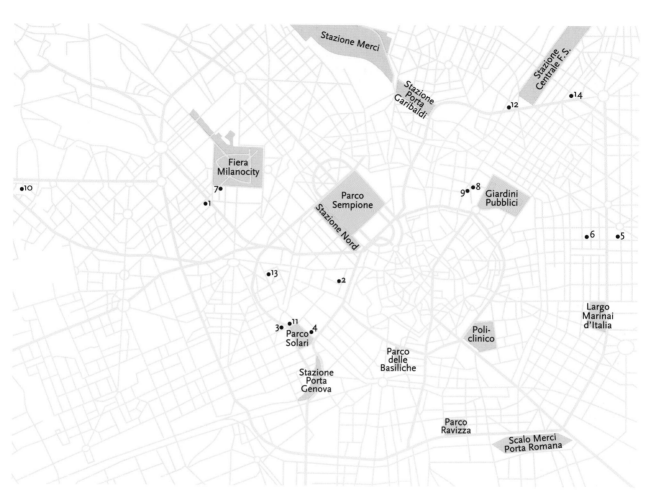

1 **Residential Building at Via Domenichino**
Via Domenichino 1-3

2 **Domus Julia, Fausta and Carola**
Via Aristide De Togni

3 **Domus Livia, Serena, Onoria, Aurelia and Flavia**
Via Letizia

4 **Domus Adele**
Viale Coni Zugna 29

5 **Domus Alba**
Via Carlo Goldoni 63

6 **Casa Marmont**
Via Gustavo Modena 16

7 **Casa Laporte**
Via Benedetto Brin 12

8 **First Montecatini Office Building**
Via della Moscova / Via Filippo Turati

9 **Second Montecatini Office Building**
Via Filippo Turati / Largo Guido Donegani

10 **Residential Quarter Harar-Dessiè for INA-Casa**
Via Harar / Via Dessiè / Via Novara

11 **Studio Ponti-Fornaroli-Rosselli and Residential Building at Via Dezza**
Via Giuseppe Dezza 49

12 **Pirelli Tower**
Piazza Duca D'Aosta 1

13 **San Francesco al Fopponino**
Via Paolo Giovio 31

14 **Montedoria Apartment and Office Building**
Via Giovan Battista Pergolesi 25 / Viale Andrea Doria / Via Mauro Macchi

Credits

Bibliography

▶ Arditi, Gloria / Serrato, Cesare: *Gio Ponti – Venti cristalli di architettura*. Venice: Il Cardo, 1994
▶ Bojani, Gian Carlo et al. (ed.): *Gio Ponti – Ceramica e architettura*. Florence: Centro Di, 1987
▶ Burg, Annegret: *Stadtarchitektur Mailand 1920–1940 – Die Bewegung des "Novecento Milanese" um Giovanni Muzio und Giuseppe de Finetti*. Basle-Boston: Birkhäuser, 1992
▶ Ciucci, Giorgio: *Gli architetti e il fascismo – Architettura e città 1922–1944*. Turin: Einaudi 1989
▶ Crippa, Maria Antonietta / Capponi, Carlo (ed.): *Gio Ponti e l'architettura sacra – Finestre aperte sulla natura, sul mistero, su Dio*. Milan: Silvana Editoriale, Cinisello Balsamo, 2005
▶ Crippa, Maria Antonietta (ed.): *Il restauro del grattacielo Pirelli*, Milan: Regione Lombardia – Skira, 2007
▶ Danesi, Silvia / Patetta, Luciano: *Il Razionalismo e l'architettura in Italia durante il Fascismo*. Edizioni La Biennale di Venezia. Venice / Milan: Electa, 1976
▶ Daprà Conti, Maria Grazia: *Una casa lunga cinquant'anni – Riscritture per Gio Ponti*. Turin: Celid, 1991
▶ Gilardi, Laura (ed.): *Gio Ponti designer*. Museo del Design Industriale Calenzano (exhibition catalogue). Florence: Alinea Editrice, 2007
▶ Green, Keith Evan: *Gio Ponti and Carlo Mollino – Post-War Italian Architects and the Relevance of their Work Today*. Lewiston / Queenston / Lampeter: Edwin Mellen Press, 2006
▶ Guarnati, Daria (ed.): *Espressione di Gio Ponti*. Monographic edition of *Aria d'Italia*, n. VIII, 1954
▶ Irace, Fulvio: *La casa all'italiana*. Milan: Electa, 1988
▶ Irace, Fulvio: *Gio Ponti a Stoccolma – L'Istituto italiano di cultura "C.M. Lerici"*. Milan: Electa, 2007
▶ Isozaki, Arata: *Gio Ponti – From the Human Scale to the Post-Modernism*. Tokyo: Seibu Museum of Art, 1986.
▶ La Pietra, Ugo: *Gio Ponti*. New York: Rizzoli, 1996
▶ Licitra Ponti, Lisa: *Gio Ponti – The Complete Work, 1923–1978*. New York: Thames & Hudson, 1990
▶ Martignoni, Massimo: *Gio Ponti – Gli anni di Stile, 1941–1947*. Milan: Abitare Segesta, 2002
▶ Miodini, Lucia: *Gio Ponti – Gli anni Trenta. Collana "Gli archivi del Progetto"*. Centro Studi e Archivio della Comunicazione dell'università di Parma. Milan: Electa, 2001

▶ Piccione, Paolo: *Gio Ponti – Le navi: il progetto degli interni navali 1948–1953*. Milan: Idea Books, 2007
▶ Ponti, Gio: *La casa all'italiana*. Milan: Edizioni Domus, 1933
▶ Ponti, Gio: *Il coro*. Milan: Uomo, 1944
▶ Ponti, Gio: *L'architettura è un cristallo*. Milan: Editrice Italiana, 1945
▶ Ponti, Gio: *In Praise of Architecture*. New York: F.W. Dodge Corporation, 1960
▶ Ponti, Gio/Libera Adalberto/Vaccaro, Giuseppe: *Verso la Casa Esatta*, Milan: Editrice Italiana, 1945
▶ Porcu, Michele / Stocchi, Attilio: *Gio Ponti – Torre del Parco e altri esagoni. Metamorfosi di un cristallo*. Milan: Abitare Segesta, 1999
▶ Porcu, Michele / Stocchi, Attilio: *Tre ville inventate*. Milan: Edizioni Charta, 2003
▶ Romanelli, Marco / Licitra Ponti, Lisa (ed.): *Gio Ponti – A World*. Milan: Abitare Segesta, 2003
▶ Stein, Axel (a cura di): *Gio Ponti 1891–1979. Obras en Caracas*. Exhibition catalogue. Caracas: Fondazione Planchart – Istituto Italiano di Cultura, 1986
▶ Tragbar, Klaus: 'Romanità', 'italianità', 'ambientismo' – Kontinuität und Rückbesinnung in der italienischen Moderne. In: Koldewey-Gesellschaft (ed.): *Bericht über die 42. Tagung für Ausgrabungswissenschaft und Bauforschung*. Bonn: Habelt, 2004, p. 72–83.

The Author

Graziella Roccella is an architect and member of the faculty of architecture at the polytechnic in Turin. Her 2005 PhD dissertation was on the subject Storia e Critica dei Beni Architettonici ed Ambientali with a work about expressionistic architecture in Italy. Presently Graziella Roccella is a lecturer in the modern history of architecure, and teaches at the Laboratorio di Progettatione Architettonica.